"Marjorie Jackson is a friend, guide, and sister whose words will encourage you, cheer you on, and, most of all, bring you closer to Jesus each day!"
—Holley Gerth, *Wall Street Journal* Bestselling Author of *You're Already Amazing*

"I love the way Marjorie speaks to real-life issues in this beautifully written devotional for young women. Renewing your mind daily in the truth of scripture and the power that comes from the Holy Spirit is truly the only way this generation will stand victorious in a culture that is resistant to the things of God. A truly captivating read for the one seeking to walk closer to Jesus."
—Gina Franzke, Director of Women's Ministry,
Cross Church, Springdale, Arkansas

"*Devoted* is one of those devotionals that will be relatable, real, and engaging for girls—encouraging them to make their relationship with Jesus their #1 priority. Marjorie's love for Jesus is highly contagious as well as her passion to help girls pursue a real and vibrant relationship with Him. I highly recommend that you get this resource in the hand of any girl in your sphere of influence!"
—Jennifer Mills, coauthor of *Salvaging My Identity* & *Even More*

"An inspiring devotional that makes you excited to spend time with your heavenly Father!"
—Olivia Hawkins, daughter of Christian comedian Tim Hawkins

"*Devoted* is scripture-saturated and covers many of the important topics that are so crucial for girls maturing into godly young women. Marjorie Jackson is wise beyond her years, and in this book she invites girls to join her on a journey of passionately pursuing the heart of God. You will not regret putting this in the hands of any young woman!"
—Meredith Floyd, wife of Pastor Nick Floyd of Cross Church Fayetteville, Arkansas

"To be a Christian woman in the world today is by no means an easy task. *Devoted* not only showcases the lies that women often buy into, but how to fight back with the Word of God. This book not only equips you with real-life applications on how to be a better Christian, but also how to defend yourself against the attacks that Satan will try to throw your way. These are life lessons that every woman should learn."
—Makensie, Hannah & Bethany Cobb, student readers

"This devotional constructs and establishes the faith of new followers in Christ, while also enriching and fortifying those whose faith is set in stone on a day to day basis."

—Ahna Cameron, daughter of actor Kirk Cameron

"Passion, encouragement, wisdom, and truth overflow from Marjorie's heart like jelly out of the yummiest peanut butter and jelly sandwich! God's very breathtaking words of beauty are convicting and inspiring at each page turn. Reading this, I humbly fall to my knees in awe of the Illustrator of my soul, and in abundant joy I can't wait for many more to be captivated by God's unconditional love in this perspective-changing and exciting read."

—Emma Mae Jenkins, popular YouTuber and Instagram personality @1corinthians13_love

"Encouraging. Convicting. Inspiring. Motiving. *Devoted* will be all of this and more for any young woman who picks up this devotional. We absolutely love Marjorie's heart for Christ and her desire to see other young women have a deep relationship with Him. We highly recommend this devotional!"

—Kristen Clark and Bethany Baird, founders of Girl Defined Ministries and authors of *Girl Defined: God's Radical Design for Beauty, Femininity, and Identity*

"Marjorie shares timeless truths from God's Word in such a beautiful, humble, and charismatic way. If you're looking to add a new book to your morning quiet time, grab this one!"

—Livy Jarmusch, author of *Secrets of Royalty* and founder of *Crown of Beauty* magazine

"Marjorie guides other young ladies to strive to become a light in this world by delving deeper into God's Word and pursuing a personal relationship with the Lord. You will definitely be encouraged to live for God and challenged to be different in this world as you read this devotional."

—Erin & Haley Jeffries, student readers

"Marjorie Jackson's pleasant writing style and sweet love for Jesus shine as she inspires you to put your focus on Him in a world seeking to conceal the truth. If you want your love for God to deepen, this uplifting read will both challenge and inspire you to seek Him with all of your heart!"

—Madyson Mesinar, student reader

"Marjorie perfectly captures the importance of being a young woman after God's own heart through this book. It boldly dives into everyday topics, problems, and struggles and gives you a different, godly perspective. It is a fantastic read and definitely one of my new favorites!"

—Abby Hutchins, student reader

Handwritten inscription:

To: Jade, First Communia. 2017.
Shalan. Ndene - Keith W.

HE IS FAITHFUL
His love Never
FAILS.
Amen.

Devoted

A GIRL'S 31-DAY GUIDE

TO GOOD LIVING

WITH A GREAT GOD

MARJORIE JACKSON

SHILOH RUN PRESS
An Imprint of Barbour Publishing, Inc.

Print ISBN 978-1-68322-166-1

eBook Editions:
Adobe Digital Edition (.epub) 978-1-68322-333-7
Kindle and MobiPocket Edition (.prc) 978-1-68322-334-4

Cover Design: Greg Jackson, Thinkpen Design
Interior Coloring Page Illustrations and Lettering: Marjorie Jackson

The author is represented by, and this book is published in association with, the literary agency of WordServe Literary Group, Ltd., www.wordserveliterary.com.

Published by Shiloh Run Press, an imprint of Barbour Publishing, Inc., P.O. Box 719, Uhrichsville, Ohio 44683, www.shilohrunpress.com.

Our mission is to publish and distribute inspirational products offering exceptional value and biblical encouragement to the masses.

Printed in the United States of America.

Contents

Introduction

The fact that I am a woman does not make me a different kind of Christian, but the fact that I am a Christian makes me a different kind of woman.

ELISABETH ELLIOT

Life is a tricky thing to navigate, and wandering around in this world aimlessly and unguarded is dangerous. Even we humans are far too complicated to decipher! We can't even figure out our own hearts. How are we ever supposed to make it here?

Truth is, we weren't made to navigate life alone. We weren't just dropped on this planet to seek out our happiness, purpose, and meaning without a clue. We don't have to live a trial-and-error lifestyle. Jesus said in John 10:10, "I came that they may have life, and have it abundantly." We can live life to the fullest by following Jesus with our whole heart and obeying His Word, the Bible.

So there's bad news and good news. . . .

Bad news first, I always say: Everyone is born missing something. It's true: *we need Jesus.* Whether we're good-as-gold girls or willfully wicked women, each one of us misses the cutoff to get into heaven—perfection. Only sinless people can get into heaven—or people with a sinless Savior on the throne of their hearts. And let me cut it straight—not one person who has ever walked this planet has been sinless—besides Jesus, that is. Good doesn't outweigh bad on God's scales. Even one sin is enough to separate us from God for eternity. No random acts of kindness, no pretty faces, no anonymous philanthropic donations can "earn" us an eternity with the Lord. We're all depraved sinners deserving of an eternity in hell, completely separated from God. This condition is a result of the fall of humankind—what happened in the Garden of Eden didn't stay in the Garden of Eden!

But here's the good news: Jesus (the Son of God *and* God in the flesh) came to earth to live a perfectly sinless life and die a gruesome, horrifying death that He didn't deserve. Jesus gave up His life for us and then He overcame death once and for all, coming back to life three days later. What did we do to deserve such an opportunity to live forever with Jesus? And not only that, but also have abundant life here on earth? The answer is this: nothing. We did *nothing*—it's all God, if only we repent of our sins and put our faith in Jesus as our Lord. We give Him our hearts, and He does the rest. I hope you've repented of your sins, put your trust in Jesus as the only One who can save you, and made Him alone the Lord of your life. But if you haven't, it's not too late. His arms are wide open, just waiting to welcome you into the family.

That, my friends, is the Gospel message—the "good news." Maybe you are already intimately acquainted with this good news—or maybe you've never heard it or accepted Jesus until now. Either way, when Jesus becomes Lord of our lives, we are His daughters! Our lives become His! We are literally giving over our hearts and lives to the God who knows how to cultivate and direct them far better than we ever could.

If our lives are now the Lord's, then everything we have belongs to Him. Every decision is made with Him. Our time, talents, money, resources, relationships, you name it—everything is God's! The "I didn't have time to read my Bible" excuse just doesn't fly anymore. *All of our time* is God's. We make time for the other stuff on our schedule, but Jesus comes first. The busiest, most hectic times of our lives are often when we need to be especially disciplined about spending time with God.

As Christians, we are called to be the salt and light of the earth (Matthew 5:13–14). That means we're supposed to stand out in stark contrast to this world, not blend in. You see, this world is under the heavy sway of the enemy of our souls (1 John 5:19). But we aren't even of this world! We're children of God (1 John 3:1). The kingdoms of heaven and this world are complete opposites. We can't live like everyone else if Jesus is truly Lord of our lives. Things have to change; we can't *help* but be different!

It's no news to me or you that everything in this world is fighting against us, trying to stop us from living for Jesus. So many distractions are tugging at us, trying to win our hearts and souls. These attacks are targeted especially at young people—we are the next generation, after all. From our relationships to entertainment to priorities to faith, we are living in a world that bombards us with lies about who we are, what we should be, and how we should become it.

Basically, we are in desperate need of truth. It's so easy to slip into wrong mindsets and believe false ideas, even as Christian girls. We can't just go with the flow; we need something solid to cling to, something constant. The Bible is the unwavering standard of absolute truth. It's the breathed Word of God. Yes, it's unpopular. Yes, it's controversial and sometimes even offensive. And yes, it can change our lives if we choose to read and obey it.

A life dedicated to serving the Lord is a life well spent. But how do we live that kind of life practically? Let's face it: we don't live in a world where God-honoring lifestyles are endorsed! And more specifically, how do we girls shine like lights for Jesus? It won't be by blending in. We can't afford to stay silent for a love so strong, a hope so real, a faith so true, and—most importantly—a heavenly Father so amazing. If we truly desire to honor the Lord in every aspect of our lives, *we will be different.*

The problem is, not many people desire to submit their lives to Jesus after counting the cost. Surrendering every facet of ourselves to Jesus' loving authority means we need to die to ourselves every single day. And dying, my friends, can be a painful process.

Dying often means sacrifice. It begins with repentance (abandoning our sins at the foot of the cross and turning away from them), but it goes so much further— it stretches into giving up our very best into God's loving control. We give Him our hopes, dreams, reputation, ideas, gifts, goals. . .you name it. No wonder the narrow road isn't a popular travel route.

That isn't a bad thing, however. On the contrary, it's a very *good* thing. You see, God has a good plan for my life and your life (Jeremiah 29:11). In fact, His plan is best, better than anything we could come up with on our best day. He wants to have a close relationship with us and guide us through life step-by-step. We don't have to wing it! With Jesus in our hearts, the Holy Spirit's counsel, and the Bible wide open, we have nothing to fear. Living life for Jesus can be amazing, adventurous, and deeply fulfilling. And that's what this book is about.

I'd like to invite you, my dear sister in Christ, to explore with me how we can draw closer to our Lord and King. Together, we'll explore many aspects of being a God-fearing, Christ-following, holiness-pursuing kind of girl. Let's learn together. Let's purpose to deepen our relationship with Him and strive to be lights so brilliant that people can't help but notice the difference Jesus makes in our lives!

How can we, as young women just barely starting out in this world, make a difference for Jesus? I'll tell you, it doesn't necessarily start off big and glamorous. You may not have a red carpet rolled out in front of you and a cheering crowd of thousands waiting to hear you share the Gospel. It may not mean starting out as a missionary overseas. Whether our opportunities to shine for Jesus present themselves as big or small, we are called to be faithful in every little thing—even in our everyday lives. In our families. With our friends. In our schools and churches. In our communities. *In our hearts.*

Let's be genuine, virtuous young women (like the woman of Proverbs 31) who fear, love, serve, worship, and proclaim the Lord with all our hearts, souls, minds, and strength. We can laugh and have fun. We can contemplate and be serious. But in all things, let's glorify the Lord, who is worthy of every ounce of our deepest praise.

Doing It All unto Jesus

Whatever you do, work at it with all your heart, as working for the Lord,
not for human masters, since you know that you will receive an inheritance
from the Lord as a reward. It is the Lord Christ you are serving.

COLOSSIANS 3:23–24 NIV

Wouldn't it be nice to live in a sitcom world—every day centering around a plot, applause and laughter for every scene, and never a dull moment? The reality, however, is that regular days bring tasks to be done, work to accomplish, laundry to fold, bathtubs to scrub, practice to make perfect. Life can feel like it's panning out to be 27 percent exciting adventure, 73 percent monotony. Sometimes we wonder when we're going to get to the real mission that God has in store for us—the good, thrilling stuff. What about taking part in mission trips, reaching the world, being a part of something huge?

Real-life example: landing a publishing deal was just about the most exciting thing that happened to me all year. It changed up my schedule a bit—I not only *got* to write a book but *had* to write a book: put words on paper, meet deadlines. And here's a secret: I wrestle with horrible writer's block. Sometimes the responsibility of the project before me can be overwhelming. I love writing, but when a blockage clogs up the brain pipes, it takes just about every remedy in existence (prayer, fresh air, coffee, Chick-fil-A, you name it) to overcome it.

The process of getting to the grand finale or finished product can often feel tedious. It's an in-between season that involves hard work, waiting, and patience. I'm not just talking about book writing here—though that's a good example of a long, but highly rewarding project. What about growing relationships, whether with family, friends, acquaintances, or coworkers? What about completing high school or college? What about training in a sport, dance, or music? There's temptation to slack off, give our B effort, or even complain when we hit a dry, rough patch. We try to simply get by, looking blessings straight in the eye and instead calling them burdens.

Most of life is spent preparing for yet another "next step." We acknowledge the importance of the big things in our lives—the book deals, the mission trips, the championships, the adventures—but maybe, just maybe, God sees it all, and it's all a crucial part of His detailed plan for us. And when you think about it, maybe that makes even the little, in-between, seemingly menial parts of our lives a *big deal* in His eyes. Maybe He's watching our faithfulness to write a thousand words, fold our little sister's laundry, scour the dishes, tutor that classmate, help Mom fix dinner, do our homework, work our summer job, run that errand. . . Forget the *maybes*. I know He does—scripture is clear that "little" is big in God's eyes.

What have you been given on your plate? Maybe it's huge. Maybe it's meager and plain—something like five loaves and two fish (Matthew 14:13–21). God works outside of our logical human understanding—He takes what we humbly offer Him and multiplies it for the kingdom of heaven. We may think we're just giving our tithe to the church, but we don't see God using that money to bless someone in need. We may think we're only babysitting, and we don't realize we're imprinting a godly example on a child who will grow up desiring to love others and know God like we do. Each little act of faithfulness can have big results. No wonder Jesus said, "He who is faithful in a very little thing is faithful also in much" (Luke 16:10). God wants the ones who have faithfully tended to His smallest responsibilities to be the ones on the big jobs—He knows they will obey and get the job done well, no matter what.

So do your best. Colossians 3:23–24 (NIV) says, "Whatever you do, work at it with all your heart, as working for the Lord, not for human masters, since you know that you will receive an inheritance from the Lord as a reward. It is the Lord Christ you are serving." In public and in private, wherever we are, whatever we're doing, we are really working for the Lord. No matter how demanding the manager, no matter how lenient the teacher, no matter how difficult the client, we respond to the Lord. He deserves our very best, our 100 percent. A cheerful heart, a thankful attitude, a joyful countenance, and diligent effort turn the daily grind into an eternal mission: bringing God glory *everywhere*. *Every day*. Through *everything*.

Are you serving? Serve like your guest is Jesus Himself. In Matthew 25:39–40 (NIV), Jesus tells us that when we serve "one of the least of these brothers and sisters," we are really serving Him. Serve others, even your enemies, all for the glory of God, like the good Samaritan from Jesus' parable in Luke 10:25–37.

Are you playing? Performing? Working? Bring your best forward. Let the gifts that God has blessed you with shine His light and openly proclaim His name. Be humble, directing the praise to the One to whom it belongs. Relying on the Lord's strength rather than your own, let Him be your "glory, and the One who lifts [your] head" (Psalm 3:3).

Are you suffering? Maybe taking a blow or two because of Jesus and His truth, or going through a tough time in life? First Peter 4:13 (NIV) encourages us to "rejoice inasmuch as you participate in the sufferings of Christ, so that you may be overjoyed when his glory is revealed." Have joy in your relationship with Christ as you trek through hardship—let your every response point back to Him. Let your patience and grace be a witness to your love for Him.

Whatever we do—and whatever we don't—we do it all for the God who has lavished us with His love and blessings. You see, good works and dos and don'ts are completely independent of our salvation—we are saved by repenting and trusting in Jesus alone. Nothing we do or don't do can save us—salvation is the work of grace alone. Jesus accepts us the way we are, however messed up we may be; He saves us, and then through His love and Holy Spirit, He changes us. He washes us clean.

The things we choose to do and choose not to do are a testimony to the Holy Spirit's sanctifying work in our lives. We live by God's Word, obey His commandments, and listen to the voice of conviction from the Holy Spirit. Some areas of conviction, aside from explicit commandments, are a little gray, and it feels like there is room for interpretation. What kinds of movies, music, media, clothing—anything—are honoring and pleasing to the Lord? First Corinthians 10:31 says, "Whether, then, you eat or drink or whatever you do, do all to the glory of God." Let the Lord lead you. Pray and seek wise counsel. If we wonder if something is pleasing to the Lord or not, we can ask, *Can I do _____ to the glory of God? Can I thank Him for this as a blessing?*

God is so good and loving toward us. He gives us His absolute best. He crafts such personalized plans for our lives. He takes great care and tends to every detail concerning us. He gave us the most wonderful gift of all for free—how can we help but give Him back our best? He deserves it more than anyone else, and His heart is warmed when His beloved children glorify Him. He sees little people like you and me offering the little that we can give, and in His power, He transforms it into something huge.

PERSONAL (OR GROUP) QUESTIONS

1. What kinds of responsibilities, opportunities, and blessings—little or big—has God entrusted you with right now?

2. When is it hardest to give your best effort? When do you feel like giving up? What is your motivation to keep going?

3. What are some decisions you have made (or would like to make) to bring glory to God through every area of your life?

Today's Challenge

You have stuff to do today, I get it. So do I. So this is not homework or an exam to see if you get to move on to the next chapter or not. Rather, here's a final charge and reminder to keep with you. Whatever you're doing today—restocking shelves, calculating algebraic formulas, working on a forehand swing, recording your debut EP album, practicing "Flight of the Bumblebee" for the upcoming recital, painting your little sister's toenails, or whatever—do it with finesse. Do it well. Do it as unto the Lord—with joy, diligence, and zero complaining or cutting corners.

Whatever you do, WORK at it WITH all YOUR heart, as working for the LORD, NOT FOR human masters, SINCE YOU KNOW THAT YOU WILL receive an inheritance FROM THE Lord AS A reward. IT · IS · THE Lord Jesus Christ YOU ARE serving.

Colossians 3:23-24

Setting an Example

*Don't let anyone look down on you because you are young,
but set an example for the believers in speech,
in conduct, in love, in faith and in purity.*
1 TIMOTHY 4:12 NIV

Did you ever get the feeling you were being watched? Well, you'd be amazed how many people are watching you and me. Not every day do you see dedicated young Christian women who actually care about living out their faith. Many people choose to disregard whatever the Bible says and just live life their own way, following their own agenda and adhering to their own style—it's true. But you know what else is true? Matthew 5:14: "You are the light of the world. A city set on a hill cannot be hidden." When we choose to shine the light of Christ and live in obedience to His Word, people take notice! People are going to see the difference Jesus makes in your life. They might ask questions. And if they like what they see and realize Jesus is the solution to their problems, they may choose to follow Him.

Contrary to what many people think, true, committed Christianity is a call to live life to the absolute fullest through Jesus (John 10:10). We are called to represent the one and only true God—how do we make Him look? I mean, if people are looking at us Christians and basing their judgments about God on what they observe in us, what do they see? Do they see a bunch of girls who don't do this and don't do that, begrudgingly following the Bible because they feel obligated?

Or do people see young women who appear to be fairly regular teens aside from a stark difference in the way we carry ourselves and behave? Do they see joy on our faces? Respect and love in our interactions? Purity in our motives and in our hearts? Do they see how we've been changed from the inside out by true love? Yes, we follow the Bible and hold to its high standards, but we're not legalistic, fake, or robotic—we're authentic about our relationship with the Lord. You'd better believe that people will watch the way we interact with our parents, siblings, friends, guys, and authority figures. They will watch what kinds of pictures we put on social media. They will watch what kinds of entertainment we choose.

But let's not be fooled: Christianity isn't a pointless list of dos and don'ts! Of course God has commandments that He requires us to follow, but they're for our own good! We aren't perfect, and we will mess up now and then, but as we strive to live a righteous life, God's grace—the undeserved favor we receive from Him—floods our lives and He sanctifies us to become more and more like Christ. The things we do and don't do are signs of our love, devotion, and obedience to Him and our trust that His Word is true and good for our lives. The dos and don'ts we follow certainly don't earn us our salvation, because we can't earn it!

First Timothy 4:12 (NIV) is the young Christian's manifesto—a burst of lively hope that our choice to follow God and His Word makes a big difference: "Don't let anyone look down on you because you are young, but set an example for the believers in speech, in conduct, in love, in faith and in purity." Right now, we're at the prime of our youth—not infants, but definitely nowhere near old. We have opportunities, mobility, and energy. Our age is a grand asset—it seems that everybody's interested in young people! Advertisements target young people as their demographic, trying to sell us whatever they can. Entertainment caters to the responses and demands of young people. In short, it's no secret that people are paying attention to us!

But what message are we sending? Is our behavior, our social media use, our relationship history, our vocabulary, our dress—you name it—worth admiring? The question is one we all need to evaluate. Thankfully, 1 Timothy 4:12 gives us a checklist—okay, so it's not actually a checklist. Truth is, if the Lord really is doing a good work within our hearts and lives, the change will be manifested through the Holy Spirit in our speech, conduct, love, faith, and purity. Let's break it down, shall we?

Speech. Some people say talk is cheap, but Proverbs 18:21 says, "Death and life are in the power of the tongue, and those who love it will eat its fruit." Our words hold great power and potential, and God doesn't take them lightly! Matthew 12:35–37 makes it clear that we are defined by and fully responsible for the words escaping our lips. Just think: our lips can pray to the Lord who can change things in the heavenlies outside of space and time. But we can also use vulgar language that may sound cool or edgy at the time but that in the end is a stain on our reputation, a negative statement about who we truly are, and an altogether bad example and testimony of someone who professes to follow Christ.

We can use our tongue to build someone up; for example, we can comfort someone going through a rough patch, speak true value into someone's life, or affirm how loved and appreciated someone is. But our tongue is also capable of abusive evil: bullying, cyberbullying, or just plain gossip—which may seem harmless but is capable of snowballing way beyond control.

When we choose to keep our words not only pure and godly, but encouraging, kind, and purposeful, the listening ears around us perk up. We share about Jesus. We openly share our faith—not in an obnoxious, abrasive, or cocky way, but rather with an inviting, joyful, and loving spirit that desires to see others draw closer to Him.

Conduct. Live with conviction. How do we present ourselves, inside and out? Do we behave authentically and honestly—being the same person in front of our friends as we are in front of our grandma—or are we two faced? People will notice inconsistencies in our lives when our walk doesn't line up with our talk. We have to keep in mind whose name we are bearing. My mom likes to remind me before I go anywhere, "You first represent Jesus, then your family, then yourself." What kind of reputation do we bear? It all plays into our testimony—the story continually being written of God's powerful, sanctifying, transforming work in us.

Love. What kind of person can possibly exhibit the selfless, unconditional love of Jesus? Surely only those who have experienced such love themselves! As Christians, we ought to exemplify the perfect love Jesus displayed for us when He gave His life so we could live free. Do we intentionally show love and kindness to people? Are we diligent in showing others through our actions and words that we love them—and more importantly, that God Himself loves and treasures them? When we really think about it, not many people do that—true, daily, enduring love stands in stark contrast to the norm.

Faith. Apathy—particularly about anything spiritual—plagues our generation. Few teenagers dare to venture beyond their own social bubbles, wants, and interests to care about eternally important matters. How many times have you heard someone say, "I'm not really into religion." *Religion?* Who said anything about that? We're in a *relationship* with Jesus Christ. We believe in Him and His Word; we love Him (but not nearly as much as He loves us!); and we desire to obey Him and serve Him because He's just so, so good! When people see us living out a vibrant faith with a true heart for Jesus—not just a church girl act—they will be intrigued. Choosing to live out our faith means choosing to swim against the crowd—the cool, the popular, the "normal." But it's worth it. When we choose to be bold, we inspire other Christians to stand up, to quit living like the world, and to start sharing their faith—and the boldness just spreads more and more contagiously from there.

Purity. You'd better believe people will watch for purity in your life. Sexuality is a big deal in our culture; where promiscuousness once would have been the hush-hush elephant in the room, it now seems that purity sticks out loudly more than ever in a world where anything and everything goes. How do we handle relationships? What kinds of movies, music, websites, jokes, and conversations do we allow and engage in? Is our dress suggestive and provocative, or modest and proper for a girl professing to have Jesus in her heart? Don't stop at appearances, though. Guarding our hearts and minds is key—because what's on the inside eventually comes out.

Set an example, says 1 Timothy 4:12. Be an influence—be someone whom others follow because they know you will lead them to where Jesus and His truth are. Encourage other believers to keep seeking the Lord and running the race with all their hearts. Inspire your brothers and sisters in Christ to live in passionate devotion to the Lord, reflected in every facet of their lives. As Christians, we are called to be leaders in doing right. Be the first to make the right decision—even if no one else will, even if no one else is watching. Be the first to double-check that fact through the scriptures. Be the first to seek God. Be the first to stand up for the truth. We lead as examples not because we are perfect or have all the answers (we don't. . .and we never will), but because we are Jesus' followers. And He is the strongest, most perfect leader of all.

PERSONAL (OR GROUP) QUESTIONS

1. Name some people in your life who look up to you. Name some people (in your life or in the Bible) who are your examples.

2. What changes for you when you realize that people are watching you even when you don't know it?

3. Of the five areas mentioned in 1 Timothy 4:12, are there any in which you have failed to be a godly example? How can you work at growing in those areas?

Today's Challenge

Evaluate your speech, conduct, love, faith, and purity.
Ask the Lord to help you be a godly example who brings Him glory.
Pray for the people who look up to you, that they may be inspired
to seek Jesus more intentionally as they observe your life.

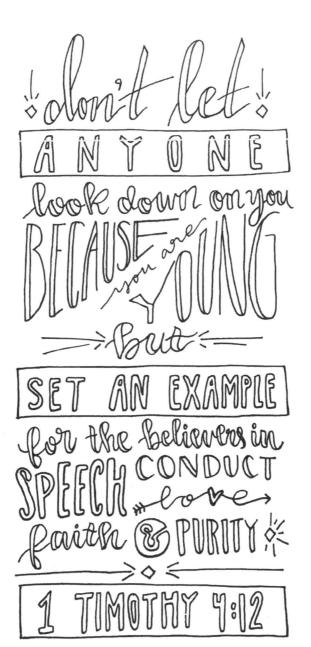

don't let
ANYONE
look down on you
BECAUSE you are YOUNG
but
SET AN EXAMPLE
for the believers in
SPEECH CONDUCT love
faith & PURITY
1 TIMOTHY 4:12

Identity

And you will be called by a new name which the mouth of the Lord will designate. You will also be a crown of beauty in the hand of the Lord, and a royal diadem in the hand of your God.

Isaiah 62:2–3

Out of all the billions of people scattered across the world, there's no one else with your exact fingerprint. You can search the world for a clone, but you'll never find someone just like you, inside or out. Not even twins. People always think my sister Genevieve is my identical twin, even though she's two years younger than me. We denied our resemblance as long as we could until realizing that some people were starting conversations with one of us and finishing it with the other, thinking we were each other! When people get us mixed up, we jokingly resort to the combined name a friend came up with for us—Marjavieve. When we both worked at Chick-fil-A, we switched name tags in an attempt to fool our coworkers. We Jackson girls may look and act alike at first glance, but stick around for five minutes and you'll realize we're each our own character. We're unique. And you know something? You're pretty one of a kind yourself.

Every day, everywhere, people ask, *Who am I?* Is it what we do? Is it who we know? Is it how we do things? The person whom we perceive ourselves to be will affect the way we carry ourselves, the way we treat ourselves, our behavior, and our choices, which means it's extremely important to know our identity! But what defines who we are? If the world is a dictionary, then there are a zillion different definitions by our names, cluttered by labels, associations, achievements, and events. There are plenty of places to *look* for our identity—but where will we *find* it? Our search could include:

- *Our activities, our performance, and our position.* You're the pastor's kid. The musical theater queen. Steve's girlfriend. The coffee barista. The best friend of the president's daughter. The shy girl. The wealthy girl. The athlete. The A-plus student. The perfect one. A member of the Jackson family. Sure, some of these things may be components of our personalities or our situations, but they hardly make up the sum total of our person. They're shaky things to stake our identity on—inconsistent, subject to change.

- *The approval of others.* The number of friends and followers we have. The tally of guys who give us attention. The pats on the back we receive from teachers and adults. The likes, comments, and compliments we get. The degree to which we resemble the world's idea of an attractive, confident woman. Our victories and wins. Searching for our identity in others will trap us forever in catering to the fickle likes and dislikes of others. People will unfriend, unfollow, reject, and move on—we'll never be able to please everybody at once: when one approves, another does not. It's a draining cycle that will leave us confused, tired, and deeply hurt.

- *Our feelings and our health.* Whoever said reality and truth aren't absolute was absolutely wrong. Reality and truth are, in fact, immovable and definite. They are *not* subject to the changing winds of our feelings. Contrary to pop culture belief, feeling like a boy does not make someone a boy. Feeling lonely doesn't mean we are unloved. Feelings fly on a whim (often with a little help from hormones). And what about sickness? Cancer, autism, Down syndrome, and the like are only surface circumstances. They can rock one's world, but they don't have the power to define a person or that person's worth.

- *Our past and our shortcomings.* The pain and hardships we've experienced. Maybe even the hurt or abuse. The struggles, addictions, temptations, and sins we've wrestled to shake off. We tend to pin the filth of our past and our sin nature to the core of our person—like sharp knives, these labels cut deepest. No matter the remorse, the repentance, the forgiveness, we can't seem to forgive ourselves. We've given ourselves a permanent, scathing review. It goes something like this: You stole something once. You regretted it, returned the item, apologized, and made things right with the people involved, and you received their gracious for-giveness. You never did it again—but you can't silence the evil voice whispering, "You're a thief." That's what guilt does—it sabotages our perception of ourselves. Like a lifeblood-sucking leech, it clings to our identity and empties our hope.

Even if we are simply tempted, we hear, "You sinner. What a failure. You can't help but sin." With such a mindset, we're likely to commit sins again and again, without ever trying to be set free.

Let's take a step back and evaluate what has become of our search. Each and every place we've looked is shallow and temporal—we cannot allow ourselves to be defined by something that will eventually fade and fall (it is our choice, after all, how we will define ourselves). If we choose to be defined by what we do, we risk losing the very thing by which we have chosen to identify ourselves. If we choose approval, then we give up our individuality and leave our perception of ourselves at the mercy (or cruelty) of others. Choosing feelings and health would be a confusing, depressing, and bumpy ride along the emotional roller coaster. Choose our past and our shortcomings, and we choose hopelessness, guilt, and a lifestyle of perpetual defeat. No—none of this will do. Every one of these identity sources ends in a crisis, because every one is built on sand.

What we need is something solid that can tell us who we really, truly are. Just because there are plenty of answers doesn't mean they're all right. Perhaps we've been asking the wrong question: It's not *what* can define us, but rather *who*. Who has the authority and the right to endow us with our true identity—the unchangeable and absolute truth about who we are?

So the whole truth and nothing but the truth? *God does.* The One who made us in the first place. Isaiah 64:8 says, "But now, O LORD, You are our Father, we are the clay, and You our potter; and all of us are the work of Your hand." Don't you think that the artist who created us should be allowed to tell us who we are? He called His creations (us!) *good* (Genesis 1:31). Even when our hearts turned from Him, even before we called upon Him to save us, Christ gave His life for us (Romans 5:8). He did it because we're worth it. Our lives matter to Him. He loves us immensely. God sees us as we truly are—*precious enough to die for.*

Who we are just gets better and better because of Jesus in us. With the Holy Spirit living in us, we are victors in battle and overcomers in temptation and trials. We are complete in Christ (Colossians 2:10). We are forgiven, and our sins are forgotten (Psalm 103:12). We are daughters of the King of kings—we're royalty, really (1 Peter 2:9). We are Christ's ambassadors (2 Corinthians 5:20). The list goes on. Our spiritual and emotional and mental health depends on our confidence in our true identity—our identity in Christ. Read it for yourself in God's Word. It will change who you are.

PERSONAL (OR GROUP) QUESTIONS

1. What are some things about you and your life that are one of a kind?
2. Where have you tried to find your identity apart from Christ, only to be disappointed?
3. Name three of God's truths that speak loudest to you about your true identity.

Today's Challenge

Take those three truths about your identity (from the third question above) and write down each one on a piece of paper, including the Bible verse to back it up (get fancy with the hand-lettering if you wish). Stick the paper somewhere you can see it often (like your mirror, door, or window) and be reminded of who you are in Christ.

and you will be called by a new name which the mouth of the Lord will designate. You will also be a Crown of Beauty in the hand of the LORD, & a Royal Diadem in the hand of your God.

Isaiah 62: 2-3

DAY 4

Joy

"Do not be grieved, for the joy of the LORD is your strength."

NEHEMIAH 8:10

Happiness—that elusive feel-goodness that always seems to be just beyond our reach. It's a blissful land where nobody's lonely, nobody's needy, and nobody's quite made it yet. Everybody's searching for it in one way or another. People have tried filling the happy void by pursuing relationships, career success, better grades, travel, money, charity, possessions, popularity, substances, a wild, carefree, adventurous life. . .you name it—but none of it seems to amount to more than disappointment and brokenness, and many times, even sin. And just when you think something will make you eternally happy and fulfill your purpose in life, you realize you're still a step away.

Looking around at the harsh, unfair world in which we live, we see cruelty, injustice, and heartbreak everywhere. What on earth can there be to smile about when such evil is rampant upon the surface of this planet we call home? Pain, suffering, and wickedness are real and thriving around every bend, it seems.

But what about us Christians? Bad things still happen, and we still feel hurt. Aren't we always supposed to be happy, since we have Jesus? Sadly, no. Never in scripture are we promised happiness as a result of following Christ. Unfortunately, happiness doesn't run as deep as we think—it's a feeling dependent on our circumstances. And if you've ever watched the news, you know that we live in a crazy world that is changing by the minute. Our circumstances can go from mountaintop highs to desperate lows in a snap. They're just not reliable enough to stake our entire emotional well-being upon—we need something more solid than just a feeling.

So there's something called joy—quite often confused with happiness, and sometimes accompanied by happiness, but very much a different quality (a fruit of the Spirit, actually), one that can stand alone on its own two feet. The difference is, joy is completely *independent* of our circumstances. Joy endures the good times and the bad, the highs and the lows, the sunny weather and the stormy days. The root of joy holds to a Rock that is strong enough to withstand fickle forecasts. But where does true joy come from?

Have you ever read the book of Philippians? It's a letter about how to be joyful in the midst of any circumstances we encounter. The apostle Paul knew that joy may coexist with sadness, pain, and hurt at times, but it never gives up because it is founded in a brilliant, exciting hope. That hope is the realization that Jesus has overcome the world (John 16:33) and disarmed the evil powers within (Colossians 2:15) so that—hey, guess what—Jesus wins in the end! Good triumphs over evil! And because Jesus lives inside of us, we win! We overcome! One day, all the tragedy, sin, and brokenness of this life will vanish along with this old earth when we are ushered into our new, eternal home (Revelation 21:4–5).

Paul explores the many characteristics of a believer's true, lasting joy: humility and selflessness (Philippians 2:3–11), a profound realization of Christ's worth (Philippians 1:21), a life set on pursuing Christ at full speed (Philippians 3:7–8), and a trust anchored in Christ's sufficiency (Philippians 4:11–13), to name only a few. Clearly, joy focuses on the bigger picture—in the light of suffering, the little picture can feel devastating. We can rest peacefully and joyfully when we trust God's grand, eternal plan for this world. As Psalm 30:5 (NKJV) reassures us, "Weeping may endure for a night, but joy comes in the morning."

Let's be real: joy is not a painkiller. Christians are not numb to sorrow and suffering; the Psalms, for instance, are a vivid example of the broad spectrum of emotions expressed by God's people. Happiness and celebration, anger and confusion, even sadness and despair sometimes occupy the heart. But joy, cultivated within us by the Holy Spirit, motivates us to not give up even when we fall down. We get back up because we have a spiritual drive and purpose for living. We live intentionally and obediently because we know it's worth it.

The enemy of our souls tries to steal our joy by lying to us, discouraging us, and getting us to fix our eyes on the waves crashing around us so that we lose faith in our ultimate source of joy. But according to 2 Corinthians 5:7, "we walk by faith, not by sight." We can sink into depression and hopelessness when we fail to realize and believe that God is good, that He is enough, that He is actively at work, and that through Him we are victorious. No matter what life looks like through our eyes, joy puts on the lenses of God's sight and helps us see circumstances through His truth, the Bible.

We can bubble over with joy because we have so much to be thankful for. It sounds cliché, but how often do we stop—especially in the middle of difficult circumstances—and count our blessings? How often do we praise the Lord out of a heart of gratitude? Do we specifically acknowledge our thankfulness in our prayers? The book of Philippians offers a few more keys to joy in 4:6: "Be anxious for nothing, but in everything by prayer and supplication with thanksgiving let your requests be made known to God."

I don't know how much or how little you have, what the dynamics of your life are, or what your situation or circumstances look like, but I know that both you and I have this to praise God for every single day: Jesus. His unmatchable love. Another day to be alive. Another day to have the honor of approaching the throne of the King of kings in prayer. Another day to serve our Master. His Holy Spirit within us. His good plans for us. First Thessalonians 5:18 (NIV) says, "Give thanks in all circumstances; for this is God's will for you in Christ Jesus." It's one of those life principles that never fails: we'll find that we enjoy life more if we demand less and are thankful for more.

Since we're discussing life principles, here's another surefire truth: comparison and jealousy will zap joy and gratitude. The latter two will fill our heart with steadfast peace and divine satisfaction, while the former two will quench any inkling of thankfulness and ultimately make us miserable. Life is not "fair" like a kindergarten teacher: just because somebody gets a lot of toys doesn't mean we will get as many. But so what? Life is more than things. Our life is not the same as somebody else's. God's plans for us are different than His plans for someone else. Philippians 3:7 is clear: "Whatever things were gain to me, those things I have counted as loss for the sake of Christ."

There it is, the fundamental truth that ties everything else in a neat bow and presents us the finished, packaged result: *Joy realizes that we have an eternal reason for celebration, endurance, faith, and hope because of Jesus.* Yes, Jesus is the key to joy! He is in us, and we are in Him. He will never leave us; rather, He is always with us (Hebrews 13:5). With God's Holy Spirit working in us, we grow fruit—joy being one of the nine delicious ones (Galatians 5:22–23). With Jesus at work in, around, and through us, we can overflow with deep, true, lasting joy—and when we think of that, how can we help but smile?

PERSONAL (OR GROUP) QUESTIONS

1. Contrast a time when you felt happy and a time when you felt profound joy.
2. What brings you joy? What reminds you of your reasons for gladness?
3. Who is an example of true joy in your life or in God's Word? What qualities stand out to you about that person?

Today's Challenge

Purpose to have joy. Resist the temptation to live in pity, guilt, or depression. Sing to the Lord and remind yourself as many times as it takes about the eternal reasons for unending celebration that we have in Jesus!

Do not be grieved, for THE JOY of the LORD is your STRENGTH

• Nehemiah 8:10 •

The Power of the Tongue

Death and life are in the power of the tongue,
and those who love it will eat its fruit.
PROVERBS 18:21

I have a confession to make: I talk too much. There, I've admitted it. As an avid chatterbox, I find it just a little too easy to keep talking after I've said enough. All the warnings in James 3 about controlling that fiery tongue? And those verses in Proverbs about knowing when to keep your mouth shut? Those are still lessons I'm learning and areas of conviction in my life. But the irony is, you don't have to be a talkative or extroverted person to have trouble controlling your tongue and watching your words. Introverts have their fair share of things to say, too.

Proverbs 18:21 says, "Death and life are in the power of the tongue, and those who love it will eat its fruit." We choose to speak life or death every time we open our mouths. The words we speak ultimately reflect what's going on inside our hearts: "The good man out of the good treasure of his heart brings forth what is good; and the evil man out of the evil treasure brings forth what is evil; for his mouth speaks from that which fills his heart" (Luke 6:45). What is the condition of our hearts? The quiet secrecy of the attitudes and thoughts within us won't last forever. Eventually, what's on the inside is going to come out through our words and our actions.

P.S., our tongue isn't limited to just words spoken out loud. Even the words we write count in the eyes of God. Remember, our words flow from our heart. Those words we text, e-mail, write, and post on social media you name the mode of messaging—God sees it all. He sees the comments we leave on posts. He reads the texts we send to that friend, to that guy. Jesus never excluded any of our methods of communication—in or out of cyberspace—when He said, "But I tell you that every careless word that people speak, they shall give an accounting for it in the day of judgment" (Matthew 12:36).

James 3:1–12 clues us in to what our tongue is all about. In fact, James says if we can control our tongue—a very difficult endeavor, indeed—we are perfect (3:2)! We're complete as we should be. We are mature. But then he goes on to describe how virtually untamable our tongue really is: "No one can tame the tongue; it is a restless evil and full of deadly poison" (3:8). Do you realize how much power we have in our tongue's hellish fire (3:6)? Just look at the kinds of evil within that little muscular organ's reach:

- *Just plain meanness.* Teenage girls have this one down to a science. For whatever reason that is fueling us—be it jealousy, flirtatiousness, anger, longing for attention or an ego boost—we are fully capable of cutting down other girls and even guys with our words. We can inflict serious burns with that flamethrower of a tongue. Online or off-line. In jest or with malicious intentions. With someone we claim to love and with someone we clearly do not. My friends, any kind of meanness is *not* of God. We should leave all malice at the cross when we are born again.

- *Gossip.* This one's big. And the problem is, it often seems very justifiable. I mean, it was just a fact, right? Or a fact that is most likely a fact. . .at least we assume it is. We never want to hurt someone's reputation or testimony—there is a difference between gossiping and sharing important information about someone with a parent or another trusted Christian adult in confidence. Spreading the latest and greatest negative news about someone to our friends, however, just spreads strife (Proverbs 6:19) and taints that person's image. I know it's interesting and satisfying to get the dirt on someone—especially someone you don't like—but know that if someone is willing to hear gossip from you or share it with you, that person is more than likely gossiping *about* you when you're not around. And gossip, though seemingly harmless, has the potential to turn into a monster. (You *did* see that *VeggieTales* episode about the rumor weed, I hope?)

- *Lying.* John 8:44 calls Satan the father of lies, which makes lying *never* okay, no matter how "white" on the scale. Proverbs 26:28 claims, "A lying tongue hates those it crushes." People who lie often will never be trusted, even when they're telling the truth. They've become a serial liar. Why should anyone who knows their record of lying believe them? Withholding the truth when it ought to be spoken is just another way to partner with the lie. Sometimes people lie with good intentions, such as to help others (Romans 3:7; Proverbs 14:25). Though their heart desires to do the right thing, the Lord is all about truth—it is 100 percent freeing (John 8:32)—and truth will always be found out in the end, either in this life or in the next. It's one of those spiritual principles: the Lord honors honesty (Proverbs 12:19).

- *Perversion.* Immorality, impurity, greed, filthiness, coarse jokes, cussing, talking about something evil—the scriptures address many ways we can, but shouldn't, be dirty with our tongues (Ephesians 5:3–12). Why become known for having an edgy vocabulary or a suggestive joke palette if those things only identify with our old self, which we put to death when we met Jesus? Not only should devoted Christ followers abstain from this kind of talk, but we should not support entertainment, jokes, or conversations that promote it.

- *Emptiness.* Manipulative flattery and meaningless chatter—they don't amount to any good. Our words have so much power—we can pray and watch God change things! Why not save our breath for when we have the opportunity to bless or encourage someone, or to speak with the Lord? We have better uses for our time, energy, and tongue.

Yikes! The decisions we make regarding our speech can send our lives in good or bad directions. A single word spoken out of line can cause endless trouble. What are we to do about this rebellious tongue of ours? James 3 makes it clear that the tongue is forever wild and free. It won't be tamed on this side of heaven, but thankfully, the Holy Spirit within us can work day by day on taming our hearts. See, if there's a direct line of communication going straight from our inside to our tongue, then we have to get to the heart of the matter, if you know what I mean.

The only way we'll see some heart change and tongue taming is by sticking to the principles found in God's Word—the powerful truth that can "judge the thoughts and intentions of the heart" (Hebrews 4:12). Search the Word for yourself, but here's a sneak peek to get you started:

- *Use discretion.* "Discretion will guard you, understanding will watch over you" (Proverbs 2:11; see also Proverbs 5:2, 11:22, 19:11).
- *Think before you speak; hold your tongue.* "Even a fool, when he keeps silent, is considered wise; when he closes his lips, he is considered prudent" (Proverbs 17:28; see also Proverbs 29:20).
- *Choose honesty.* "Truthful lips will be established forever, but a lying tongue is only for a moment" (Proverbs 12:19).
- *Speak humbly.* "You rebuke the arrogant, the cursed, who wander from Your commandments" (Psalm 119:21).
- *Honor others.* "Let no unwholesome word proceed from your mouth, but only such a word as is good for edification according to the need of the moment, so that it will give grace to those who hear" (Ephesians 4:29).
- *Honor and glorify God.* "Praise the LORD! Praise the LORD, O my soul! I will praise the LORD while I live; I will sing praises to my God while I have my being" (Psalm 146:1–2).
- *Choose life.* "But the word is very near you, in your mouth and in your heart, that you may observe it. See, I have set before you today life and prosperity, and death and adversity" (Deuteronomy 30:14–15).

Why do words matter? Who even cares what comes out of our mouths? Well, God does. In the light of scripture, words are very powerful; words lead to action and change. Look just three verses into the Bible (Genesis 1:3): "Then God said, 'Let there be light'; and there was light." Words are meaningful and are not to be used flippantly. One's word is to be kept. We can be sure that when God speaks, He keeps His Word: "He who promised is faithful" (Hebrews 10:23). Words make a difference. Words can tear down and crush people whom the Lord loves, but they can also be the catalyst to spur the greatest thinkers and world changers into action. Words can usher someone into the darkest place that person has ever been, or words can spread the light of the Gospel. Words can fly like bullets at the wrong enemy, or we can fight the right spiritual battles with our prayers. So may you and I, as devoted followers of the Lord, speak life—because words matter a whole lot.

PERSONAL (OR GROUP) QUESTIONS

1. When do you have the most trouble filtering your words and controlling your tongue? What is your main shortcoming in taming your tongue?

2. Think of the most impactful thing anyone has ever said to you. What was your reaction or response? How does this attest to the power of words?

3. Think of three people whom you can lift up with your words this week. How can you learn to purposefully choose words of life over death?

Today's Challenge

Think before you speak. Write down James 1:19: "Everyone must be quick to hear, slow to speak and slow to anger." Intentionally practice filtering and choosing your words wisely today so that they will be tactful, true, and honoring to the Lord.

Prayer

The prayer of a righteous person is powerful and effective.
JAMES 5:16 NIV

I hope you saw the movie *War Room*. It's a powerful reminder that prayer matters and makes a big difference. Oftentimes, prayer is a full-out *fight* against the enemy that we wage with God on our side by using His armor (found in Ephesians 6:10–18) to fight lies and darkness with truth and light. Ephesians 6:12 makes it clear: "Our struggle is not against flesh and blood, but against the rulers, against the powers, against the world forces of this darkness, against the spiritual forces of wickedness in the heavenly places." James 5:16 (NIV) reminds us, "The prayer of a righteous person is powerful and effective." *Prayer works.*

Prayer is also one of the ways we draw closer to God. It's humbling to realize we have the honor of approaching the throne of our heavenly Father and actually conversing with Him—and the best part is, He's listening and responding! He is elated to hear our voice (Song of Solomon 2:14). We bring our praises, our joys, our requests, our hurts, our questions before Him, and we watch things happen. We watch our relationship with God grow and strengthen.

There's no secret formula or proper order of words to make prayer happen—skip the Thees and the Thous if you wish. We revere Him, we worship Him, we marvel over His great power as King—and we rest, we relax, and we enjoy His company as friend. We talk to God because He loves us and wants us to involve Him in our lives. He'll do amazing things in us, around us, and through us if we let Him.

If you're like me, you don't always find it second nature to pray about everything. I mean, many people are in the habit of praying before they chow down on their food, but just about every other prayer time takes some level of discipline. We send sweet notes that say things like "Praying for you!" to our friends and family, but when do we *actually pray for them*?

And even more, what is our first response? When that doctor report comes, do we pray, or do we first work ourselves up into a frenzy of worry? When our relationships are in turmoil, do we pray, or do we take matters into our own hands (and potentially make life harder than it was five minutes before we did)? When our day isn't going the way we planned, do we pray, or do we fret and fume in anger over the traffic, long lines, annoying people, barking dogs, or even God?

Holocaust survivor Corrie ten Boom put it wisely: "Is prayer your steering wheel or your spare tire?" I'd like to say steering wheel, but if I'm really honest. . . Do we wait until life is at its worst—until tragedy strikes—before we pull out the most powerful weapon we've been given to defeat darkness and invite God's intervention in our life? It's time that we Christians started being intentional about our communication with the Lord. Here are three creative ideas to grow your prayer life:

- *Pick prayer targets.* My friend Madyson and I decided to hold each other accountable regarding praying deliberately. We chose certain everyday activities and picked specific things to pray about while we do them. Here's what that looks like: When we brush our teeth, we pray for our pastor and church. When we do the dishes, we pray for our siblings. When we do laundry, we pray for our parents. And when we put on makeup (or just get ready in the morning), we pray for our future husband. Picking prayer targets and keeping each other accountable has been a tremendous reminder to pray even as I go about my regular day.

- *Write a letter to God.* I love good old-fashioned letters. Sometimes I'll write God a letter in my journal. It helps me get my thoughts down on paper and bring them into focus as I lay them before the Lord. When I sort out those cares and concerns before the Lord, I can think more clearly and pay more attention to what the still, small voice of the Holy Spirit may be trying to speak to my heart in a quiet moment or through God's Word. Writing prayers and prayer requests, praises, and answers is also a good way to document the work God is doing in your life. We can't deny that God loves us or is involved in our lives when we have clear (written!) proof that He is faithful!

- *Make a weekly list.* Here's another idea I have tried: at the beginning of each week, I would make a list of specific prayer points for that week, and then each day (either at a set prayer time or in a quiet moment) I would go down the list, praying for each specific thing. I listed all my siblings and my parents, two friends (I would usually pick different ones each week), my future husband, the future, and just about anything else I could think to pray for. It kept me on track with praying for specific, relevant needs.

Finally, don't forget to praise the Lord and thank Him for His blessings, His goodness, and who He is! We should pray about our needs instead of worrying, knowing that God desires to help us and draw us closer to Him. But praying isn't the same as making a Christmas list. Just as we would converse with any friend, we bring our praise, our conversation, and our needs to the Lord and thank Him for always being there for us. Also, ask the Holy Spirit what *His* prayer list for you looks like! What does He want you to pray about? He's the One sitting on the throne, after all. Pray a prayer to the God whom we serve, and amazing things will happen.

PERSONAL (OR GROUP) QUESTIONS

1. What motivates you to pray? When do you find it hardest to pray?
2. What are some stories from scripture and from your own life that have strengthened your faith in the power of prayer?
3. What are some other ways you can pray and/or establish the habit of prayer in your life?

Today's Challenge

Try one of the three suggested prayer ideas: pick some prayer targets, write a letter to God, or make a prayer list.
Talk to God—but don't forget to listen!

The prayer of a righteous person is powerful + effective.

James 5:16

Why Read the Bible?

For the word of God is living and active and sharper than any two-edged sword, and piercing as far as the division of soul and spirit, of both joints and marrow, and able to judge the thoughts and intentions of the heart.

HEBREWS 4:12

We all have problems. We all have questions. We all need hope, encouragement, and a little direction. I might have some answers to help you, and you might have some answers to help me, but let's face it—nobody has *all* the answers. Nobody, that is, except God, the Creator of the universe, the inventor of knowledge, wisdom, and understanding, and the ultimate truth. He placed us here on earth with a grand purpose but with no guarantees that life would be easy (it's not). Thanks to our flawed human nature, living life can be rather hard. Being a godly, different-from-the-rest-of-this-fallen-world kind of woman can seem like a nearly impossible task—right up there next to licking your elbow. (Did you try it? You can't do it!)

God did, however, leave us with the Bible. Don't judge that leather-bound book by its cover—within its pages lies the story of humanity since the creation of the world; the inspired words straight from God's mouth; a detailed and specific manual for living life; and one of God's direct sources of communication with us. It's also His divine, enrapturing love letter to us; the absolute, unwavering standard of truth; and the unchanging revelation of God and His heart toward us and toward right and wrong. Times will change, culture will change, life will change—but the Word of God will forever (and ever) be the same (Isaiah 40:8).

We must hold up everything—in our lives and in the world—side by side with the scriptures to see if it lines up with the truth: actions, thoughts, words, feelings, relationships, ideas, media, entertainment, you name it. That includes Christian books (even the one you're reading!), movies, celebrities, musicians—yes, even pastors, churches, and sermons need to be scrutinized under the brilliant light of God's infallible Word. Checking, double-checking, questioning, and affirming is not paranoia—it's what we would call "being like a Berean" in church lingo. Just like the people of Berea from Acts 17:10–11, we listen to preaching (and the like) with God's Word at the forefront of our minds, filtering truth from untruth, biblical fact from churchy fluff, substance from emotional hype. We don't want to be influenced by anything that is not endorsed by Christ (Colossians 2:8).

If we allow the Holy Spirit to teach us and guide us in wisdom, He will bring the Bible to life for us. The Word of God written on our hearts (Jeremiah 31:33) will begin to be downloaded into our minds and manifested in our actions and lives as we soak in the purest truth. "Then you will know the truth, and the truth will set you free" (John 8:32 NIV)—free from the lies and bondage and mental traps we've bought into. Free from the deceptions and chains of culture and pressure to conform to the world. Free from identity crises and questions of purpose. Free from evil and impurity in our hearts. Verses will pop off the page, shouting directly to what we're going through in life.

Reading God's Word is spiritual nourishment. Just as we need food to sustain our physical bodies, we need the Word of God to feed, grow, and maintain a healthy spiritual life. When we are spiritually malnourished, we feel the effects of our sickly spiritual eating habits. It's all too easy to respond out of our natural human impulses (the flesh) rather than conducting our behavior in the God-honoring way (the Spirit) we are called to as Christians.

Verses like Ephesians 4:24 and Colossians 3:10 talk about "putting on the new self." That means bringing about this "new self" requires action and effort on our part—it's not just a magical change that happens overnight along with salvation. Let me tell you, there's no better way to throw off the old girl (the flesh-gratifying, impulse-pursuing, pre-salvation person we were before Jesus transformed us) and put on the new girl (the Spirit-walking, Christ-transformed, post-salvation person we are from the moment Jesus enters our lives) than by saturating our minds and hearts in God's spiritual grow food.

Before I make the Bible sound like it's all about you and me. . .it isn't. It's written *for* us to help us learn more about God and how He has worked in lives, is working in lives, and will work in lives. The Bible as a whole is the grandest (and truest) story in all the world about the history of humanity and God's intimate involvement in the lives of His people. You know how in other religions people are trying to forge a path to reach "God"? Well, the one true God is unique in that He was the first to extend His powerful hand and reach out to people; He is the One who made a path for us to reach Him. That's the thesis of the Bible right there. So the Bible is about God. Period.

I absolutely love this vivid quote by E. Stanley Jones: "The Bible will be self-authenticating to you. It will find you at your deepest depths. You will know it is inspired, for you will find it inspiring. You will know God has gone into it, for God comes out of it. It is a revelation, for it reveals. It is an inexhaustible mine. You think you have exhausted it, and then you put down the shaft of meditation and strike new veins of rich ore."*

We'd be crazy to miss out on the book penned by God Himself. Not to mention, it's nearly impossible to live by His Word if we've never read it. He has given us all truth at our fingertips, a clear view into who He is and what He has done (and is doing), and a compelling letter from Him to ourselves that defines who we are and how loved and full of potential we are. I am convinced that in order for us Christians to grow in our walk with Christ, live like Jesus commands, and thrive as we proclaim Christ in this world we live in (but don't belong to—John 17:16), we must be intentional, disciplined, and tenacious about reading and meditating on the Word consistently. Every single day. But how? It's easier said than done. So stay tuned! We'll get to that in a future devotional.

*E. Stanley Jones, *The Way to Power and Poise,* (Nashville: Abingdon, 1970).

1. What are some of the ways God has spoken to you directly from His Word?

2. Why is it important to keep God's Word as the ultimate standard and truth? How have you seen this to be true in your own life, in culture, and in the world?

3. Why is it important to get the Word of God inside us? How do you benefit spiritually from reading God's Word?

Today's Challenge

Pick a book of the Bible to stick to, reading a chapter or two a day. Whatever book or section of the Bible you choose, it's all part of God's inspired Word—and there's so much to learn and to grow from along the way.

For the WORD of GOD is living & active & sharper than any 2-edged sword & piercing as far as the DIVISION of soul of both joints & marrow & spirit, & able to judge the thoughts + intentions of the ♡.

Hebrews four:12

How to Read the Bible

Fix these words of mine in your hearts and minds; tie them as symbols on your hands and bind them on your foreheads. Teach them to your children, talking about them when you sit at home and when you walk along the road, when you lie down and when you get up. Write them on the doorframes of your houses and on your gates.

DEUTERONOMY 11:18–20 NIV

From the moment we give our lives to Christ, we change. Our citizenship is transferred to heaven. Jesus dethrones whatever or whoever else was ruling our heart and He becomes Lord—the new boss. But not all change is instantaneous or overnight. People have coined the term *baby Christian* (a new Christian), but quite honestly, none of us will ever "arrive" in this life. We'll never have it all together. We will always—*must* always—be growing. As with any living thing, growth is a sign of health.

But we only kid ourselves into believing we'll grow if we aren't proactive about reading the Bible—getting "fed" with our spiritual food. I can't stress enough the importance of making a habit of reading the Bible regularly. No matter what our spiritual walk looks like at any given point, we need to be delving into the Word every single day, praying and meditating on what the scriptures say so we can grow and deepen our relationship with God.

When I was thirteen, I made the decision to read the Bible every single day for the rest of my life. Think that sounds daunting? Think again. Pretty soon after, grabbing my Bible and reading for five or so minutes became sheer habit— part of my bedtime routine. Many times at that point in my life, however, I would read the Bible just to check it off my to-do list. I knew it was important, but I just wasn't feelin' it, you know?

That commitment to daily Bible reading was one of the best decisions of my life, however. I would challenge everyone to make the same decision—to make time for God and His Word every single day (Psalm 132:4–5). Friends, no matter how "boring" we may perceive the Bible to be at times, God is always trying to speak to us. And sometimes He gets a busy line—we're distracted by life and oblivious to the fact that He has a message for us.

Boredom is merely a sign that maybe we're not listening—maybe we're not hearing His voice coming out of those pages like we should. Or maybe we're not understanding. In these moments, we can turn to Jesus and pray that He would open our hearts to hear and understand a word from Him. With the help of the Holy Spirit, we can glean "teaching, rebuking, correcting and training in righteousness, so that [we] the servant[s] of God may be thoroughly equipped for every good work" (2 Timothy 3:16–17 NIV). Sometimes conviction stings as it strips us of sins we have been holding on to, but we also experience a warm joy knowing that God corrects us because He loves us (Proverbs 3:12). We must be broken and teachable when we come before God and His holy Word. And nothing brightens a day more than specific encouragement from the Lord that comes at just the right moment! (God has a way of doing that.)

So let's talk about having a quiet time. Everybody does their quiet time differently; it may be quiet or not so much. "Quiet" time is simply time when we shut out the world, quiet our minds, and detox from life's stress by spending time with the Lord, intentionally focusing on listening to His voice. He is our God, our Savior, and our best friend, after all. Prayer, Bible reading, worship, journaling, even artwork—all can be part of a quiet time routine. And who says there even has to be a routine? Routine is good for discipline and habit-forming purposes, but we don't need to confine the Holy Spirit to a fixed A-B-C process. I'm all for having a routine, so long as it doesn't become a religious ritual checklist. This is relationship time—a time set apart to be in the presence of God.

Let's focus on reading the Bible, because everything else we do revolves around that. I mean, if it isn't found in the Bible or in harmony with it, then we probably shouldn't be doing it. The Word of God is truly so important; it holds so much more weight and value than anything else (Psalm 139:17). We can't afford but to know it as intimately as we possibly can.

That is why we must meditate on it day and night (Psalm 1:2). To meditate on God's Word is to ponder it deeply, struggle with it, and let it fully sink in. We need to digest the words we read, breaking down each verse into its elements, takeaways, context, truths, and applications. We need to consciously acknowledge the relevance, the superiority, the validity, and the significance of God's Word over anyone else's.

Deuteronomy 11:18–20 (NIV) reads, "Fix these words of mine in your hearts and minds; tie them as symbols on your hands and bind them on your foreheads. Teach them to your children, talking about them when you sit at home and when you walk along the road, when you lie down and when you get up. Write them on the doorframes of your houses and on your gates." Letting the Word of God pervade our everyday lives invites true change and sanctification to occur. As Jesus says in John 17:17, "Sanctify them in the truth; Your word is truth."

I love sermons and Christian books and podcasts, but never let supplementary Christian resources, ministries, or even leaders replace the Bible or even interpret the Bible for you in a way that does not align with the truth of scripture. By all means, let's seek to enrich our understanding of the scriptures through Bible study tools and good talks about the Bible, but know that God's Word is firm and it forever will stand above all (Psalm 119:89).

Though I'm not too consistent, I do like journaling alongside my Bible reading. Keeping track of what God is doing in my heart and in my life; writing prayers, prayer requests, and praises; taking notes in church and on podcasts; and writing my own commentaries regarding what I read in the Bible are some of the reasons I keep a Bible journal. It's good to never forget what God is doing and has done in your life!

Bible reading is a subject I'm passionate about. In fact, when I was fifteen, I wrote a book, *The Greatest Book You've Never Read*, with the intention of getting other young people my age excited about reading the Bible. A lot of times I get funny comments about the title, like, "So after I've read your book, it becomes

The Greatest Book You've Ever Read, right?" The truth is, not my book or any other book can compete with the Bible. It is truly a gem—a masterpiece straight from the greatest Author you'll ever meet.

PERSONAL (OR GROUP) QUESTIONS

1. What sorts of tips have you found helpful in your own quiet time?
2. What distracts you from fully focusing on the Lord? What helps direct your focus back?
3. What are some ways you have benefited from filling your mind and life with scripture?

Today's Challenge

Memorize the coloring verse, Deuteronomy 11:18–20. Write it down, repeat it, study it, sing it, rap it, hand-letter it, color it. Ingrain it in your head and heart, and ask the Lord to give you the discipline you need to regularly memorize His truth.

---

50 | MARJORIE JACKSON

FIX THESE WORDS of MINE
IN YOUR ♡s & MINDS.

tie them as symbols on your hands & BIND THEM on your foreheads♡

Teach them TO YOUR children TALKING about THEM WHEN YOU sit @ home Walk ALONG THE ROAD LIE down get UP

WRITE THEM on the

DOORFRAMES

of your HOUSES & ON YOUR gates

Deuteronomy 11:18-20

Why Share Your Faith?

For I am not ashamed of the gospel, because it is the power of God that brings salvation to everyone who believes.

ROMANS 1:16 NIV

The Gospel: that gloriously great news that God loved us so much that He sent His Son to die for our sins and overcome death. If we receive this free gift by putting our trust in Jesus as our Lord and Savior, we can live forgiven, redeemed, free, and hopeful, with an eternity awaiting us in heaven with Him. Every Christian knows this thrilling message—it's what saved us, after all! We accepted it and were made new. We were born again: once physically, now spiritually. It's the drive behind our love and obedience to Jesus. It gets better—we get God's Holy Spirit living inside of us as a Helper! He is the reason we can live out our faith. He empowers us and guides us with His sweet presence.

And now we have the wildest, most dangerous, most amazing mission ever: God Himself has given us the high honor and responsibility of representing Jesus (Ephesians 6:19–20) and sharing this Gospel of truth with the world. Remember the Great Commission in Matthew 28:19–20? We tell *everyone* about Jesus. His grace, His forgiveness, and His love are for even the most serially wretched sinners and for the "good guys next door" who never realized they needed a Savior.

God's Word goes on to describe this mission: yes, tell everyone—but also teach, disciple, and encourage them in their new (or not-so-new) faith. We are to live each moment, in front of crowds and behind closed doors, as the daughters of the King we are, seeking to fulfill our heavenly mission so that we may bring glory to our Lord.

Being an ambassador for Christ (2 Corinthians 5:20) is a powerful role.

People are going to be verifying our authenticity, examining our lifestyles, and making judgments based on their observations of us about what God and Christianity are really all about. They will be scrolling our social media feeds, watching our interactions with family and friends, listening to the words in our vocabulary, and mentally archiving the things we do and don't do. They will take note of if and when we fall—and if and how we recover.

People want to know if Christians are two-faced, wishy-washy hypocrites. They've seen plenty of people who talk one talk but then walk another walk. But what about us? No, we're not perfect by a long shot. But we do serve a perfect Lord who desires for us to surrender every part of our being to Him so that He can use us in amazing ways to reach others. He can use us to share our faith with unbelievers and stand alongside them as they make Jesus their Lord and Savior. He can use us to encourage people who are weak or struggling in their faith and to set the tone for a relationship or conversation. God can use us to encourage other like-minded Christians. There is no limit to what God can do, and I've learned firsthand that the kinds of things God has in store are rarely imaginable!

Choosing to be God's vessel (2 Timothy 2:20–21) to bless and minister to others is a truly fulfilling joy. We're in our element, because a vessel is literally what we were created to be! Sharing the Gospel, making disciples, encouraging others toward Christ—isn't that what missionaries do? Correct. You and I and every other Christ follower are missionaries. We don't need to go overseas—we don't even need to leave our city—to share the Gospel with unbelievers. Of course, I'm all for going on mission trips, and I hope you get many opportunities to take part in them. But that doesn't change the fact that we are living square in the middle of a mission field.

Look around. Our mission field is just as real as the ones in the heart of the jungle and in oppressive countries ruled by tyrannical leaders. Take school, work, sports, Walmart, even church: real people with real lives, real sins, real struggles, real souls headed for a real place called hell are in desperate need of Jesus. There are people everywhere, Christians and non-Christians, who need help, encouragement, and a substantial hope to cling to. People who need God's love, truth, joy, and vibrant life splashed all over their weary selves. God has things to say to these people, hope to give them—and you and I can be the ones who say to the Lord, "Here am I. Send me!" (Isaiah 6:8).

Our lives should be in harmony with the Gospel we claim to bear. Let your life share the good news—but don't forget to use words, too! Whether we're street witnessing, sharing about Jesus with an unsaved friend, discipling a new Christian, ministering to a fellow believer, or simply standing up for what we believe, keep in mind God's heart for this lost, broken, sinful world: He doesn't want a single one to perish (Matthew 18:14; 1 Timothy 2:3–4). While some may reject the Gospel and the opportunity to be saved, John 4:35 (NIV) tells us, "Open your eyes and look at the fields! They are ripe for harvest."

So many people are ready to receive the Gospel; we just have to break through the "awkwardness" of talking about things that actually matter (such as the eternal fate of their soul) and be bold about sharing the truth. Heads up: the truth—especially the Gospel—is frequently offensive, no matter how lovingly it is presented. Why do you think there is persecution? People don't like being wrong. They don't like confronting sin. They don't like the thought that if they're wrong about not being wrong, they could end up in a place called hell that they hope is not real. They may snap into defensive mode to combat what they perceive as "hate"—and who likes being labeled a "hater"?

But here's the truth: those offended by the Gospel have the definition of "hate" all wrong. Ephesians 4:15 talks about speaking the truth in love. By no means should the truth be used to demean a person whom God has created. Rather, "love must be sincere. Hate what is evil; cling to what is good" (Romans 12:9 NIV). True love will rejoice with the truth (1 Corinthians 13:6), but hate would altogether *not care* and hold it back. Hate would be knowing there is a real hell where those separated from God by sin will go unless they repent of their sins (which they *do* have, because we've *all* sinned) and trust in Jesus. . .and doing nothing about it. It's in our power to speak the truth—we have the means to, we have the opportunity, and the Holy Spirit is prompting us—but we just don't care enough about their soul to say a word. We let them wallow in sin.

Friends, *hate* is withholding the truth when we have the power to share with others what could set them free. Whether we're talking about someone in a sinful lifestyle such as cohabitation or homosexuality, or simply about Jesus as the only way to be saved, we must speak the truth. The truth may be hard, unpopular, offensive, intolerant, and absolute, no matter how much love and kindness it is smothered in. But the truth is sanctifying (John 17:17), and God's truth is the only thing that will set people free (John 8:32).

I believe sharing our faith is one of the most exciting adventures God places in our lives. Bearing the truth of the Gospel is a beautiful thing. Romans 10:13–15 says, "For 'Whoever will call on the name of the Lord will be saved.' How then will they call on Him in whom they have not believed? How will they believe in Him whom they have not heard? And how will they hear without a preacher? How will they preach unless they are sent? Just as it is written, 'How beautiful are the feet of those who bring good news of good things!' "

PERSONAL (OR GROUP) QUESTIONS

1. How has the Gospel changed you?
2. What apprehensions keep you from sharing the Gospel?
3. What is your motivation to tell others about Jesus? Where can you start this week?

Today's Challenge

Ask the Lord to bring to mind someone He has placed in your life with whom you can have a Gospel conversation. Maybe it's the server at the restaurant, the grocery store clerk, a coworker, your cousin, your classmate. Pray that God places a burden on your heart for the lost.

ROMANS
ONE
SIXTEEN

For I am NOT ASHAMED of the Gospel

because it is the POWER OF GOD

that brings salvation to EVERYONE who believes.

Defending Your Faith

But sanctify Christ as Lord in your hearts, always being ready
to make a defense to everyone who asks you to give an account
for the hope that is in you, yet with gentleness and reverence.
1 Peter 3:15

Never lose your awe over what Jesus willingly suffered on the cross for us—and the victory He won over evil. Never let the Christian clichés or familiarity taint the beauty of the greatest act of love that ever was. Never become numb to the reality that we are daily surrounded by hell-bound souls who need to be set free by the truth of the Gospel. I've fallen prey to the "good Christian" trap before: I get "into" witnessing, "into" missions, "into" the Gospel. But evangelism—sharing the Gospel—is not a fad, activity, or sport. It's not just a tract, bumper sticker, social media bio, or something we do on mission trips. After what Jesus did for us? For everyone? Sharing the Gospel becomes a lifestyle—a lifelong calling, mission, and priority. We must share with everybody the Gospel that has captivated us, saved us, and changed our eternity—and can change theirs, too! But where does the conversation start?

Have you ever wondered, *Who do I talk to? How do I bring up the subject? What do I say? What will they say? What if they ask a question and I don't know the answer? What if they say something that rocks my faith?* So many unknowns, so many worst-case scenarios. . . Well, let me share some of the things I've learned as I've explored these questions myself, one friend to another.

First Peter 3:15 says, "But sanctify Christ as Lord in your hearts, always being ready to make a defense to everyone who asks you to give an account for the hope that is in you, yet with gentleness and reverence." As with anything in life, preparation makes sharing our faith less nerve wracking. We have a faith built on solid Rock—there are answers and explanations to tough questions. The truth of God's Word is timeless and unshakable. We have a faith worth researching, defending, and knowing well—not because God needs defending, but because often people are in need of answers to their tough questions that keep them from believing the Gospel. Sometimes we need affirmation of what we believe.

The study of *why* we believe what we believe is called "apologetics"—all the arguments for the existence of God, the resurrection of Jesus, the validity of the scriptures, the proof of intelligent design versus evolution, and so on. I highly recommend studying up on some of the hot-topic questions we hear around us. Such study not only will equip us to better answer tricky questions but also will strengthen our faith in the process.

Disclaimer, though: facts, though they can change minds, cannot change hearts. We can share the Gospel and preach the truth from dawn till dusk, but at the end of the day, we cannot "convert" a single person. We don't have the kind of power over people's hearts that can draw them to repentance and true, lasting change. The Holy Spirit does the real work within people's hearts (John 14:17)—we're just blessed to be a part of it!

First Corinthians 1:18 proves it: "For the word of the cross is foolishness to those who are perishing, but to us who are being saved it is the power of God." Those who don't accept it or understand it—they think it's just crazy. I mean, God Himself loves us that much? He did that? But is it worth giving up every-thing to follow Him? *No way. Yes way? Really?* It's just too hard to believe and comprehend without the Holy Spirit's help. Their spiritual eyes and ears are not ready to recognize the truth that would revolutionize their entire destiny (see Matthew 13:5–6). Relying on the Holy Spirit is *key*. Tracts and pamphlets can be great tools or conversation starters, but we can also use them as cop-outs from personally spending time talking with someone toward whom God is nudging us. No, we don't have all the answers, but the Lord does. Let the Holy Spirit guide you to those He wants you to talk to. Street witnessing is great if the Lord inspires you to do that, and He can and does use that kind of ministry, but also consider that there are people who regularly cross your path who need to hear His good news.

First things first: *Know the Bible!* Become intimately familiar with the Gospel— I once heard a youth pastor challenge his students to preach the Gospel to themselves in the mirror every morning. If someone asked you how to be saved, what would you say? Know your testimony—it is one of your greatest assets, because it is your personal story about what God has done for you, and nobody can deny that. Ephesians 4:14–15 says, "We are no longer to be children, tossed here and there by waves and carried about by every wind of doctrine, by the trickery of men, by craftiness in deceitful scheming; but speaking the truth in love, we are to grow up in all aspects into Him who is the head, even Christ." Knowing God's Word anchors us in the truth. When doubts try to shake our faith, we stand firm in what we know to be true.

There are zillions of different religions and belief systems out there—but only one is the truth. In life, we will have many opportunities to forge friendships and share the Gospel with people who have diverse beliefs. Without agreeing with them, we can learn to kindly and gently ask questions, respectfully challenge their views with questions to get them thinking about the flaws in their belief, and humbly present to them the truth about God's loving sacrifice and what it means for them. Show love without *ever* compromising the truth (speak the truth in love, as we read in Ephesians 4:15). People aren't "dumb" for believing something false; they are deceived. They are lost and need to be found. They are in darkness and we can point them to the light! First John 5:19 (NKJV) points out, "We know that we are of God, and the whole world lies under the sway of the wicked one." The enemy will try to discourage us from spreading the truth, because we're attacking the deception he has worked so hard to establish. Contrast these two stories:

When I was fifteen, I went street witnessing with some friends at a farmers' market. It was my first time ever to share the Gospel—and who should be my first conversation partner but the meanest woman I've ever met (I'm sorry, but it's true!). What started as three young girls sweetly asking Gospel questions to an older woman ended with three shocked girls (me in tears) being angrily told they were "judgmental," "closed minded," and "brainwashed." She believed *everyone* went to heaven—Hitler included—no matter what. She was highly offended by our "dogma." Do you think I ever wanted to witness again after nearly being devoured alive at the farmers' market? Nope, you bet not.

But thank the Lord, I had been bracing myself for an attack from the enemy. When God is doing great work through His children, the devil will do anything in his power to thwart it. I did continue to share the Gospel after that nightmare experience, and two years later I had the best conversation of my life. Headed back home from an El Salvador mission trip, I was pumped and inspired to share the Gospel back in the States, even on the airplane ride home. So I chatted with the sweet lady sitting next to me. Kind and curious, she poured out her life and her questions on me—a young teen girl whose name she didn't even know—about prayer, guilt, church, understanding the Bible, and salvation. I tried my best to answer her questions, but it kind of felt like we were going in circles. She didn't seem to understand that she couldn't earn salvation—that it was through Jesus, through God's grace alone, not through her good works!

Finally, I sat back. There was an awkward pause. The lady reached her hand out toward me and asked, "So. . .how do I get Jesus?" She teared up as she smiled. "There is a lump in my throat, and I feel like I am going to cry." I can't even begin to describe my elation. I did *nothing* to "convert" her, but God graciously used me to help her through some questions and to listen to her stories as a caring friend. That plane ride home, this woman—whose name I never caught until the end of our conversation—became our sister in Christ. It's worth pressing on, even when you encounter a bad experience or two. Friends, nothing in life is more fulfilling than obeying the Lord.

A final thought: What happens when we, as Christians, have doubts about our faith? I've been there—it's frightening and confusing—but there is hope. In fact, don't be afraid of questions, because there are *answers*. And I found the ones I needed—not only the logical explanations, like in apologetics, but answers for the spiritual side of things. Here are two prayers, straight out of God's Word, to pray when struggling with doubts: "I do believe; help my unbelief" (Mark 9:24), and "Increase [my] faith" (Luke 17:5). Our faith isn't based just on facts or what is seen, but we have faith in what is unseen (Hebrews 11:1; 2 Corinthians 4:18) and in the relationship we have cultivated with the Lord.

I know I haven't covered, nor do I know, everything there is to know. Sharing the Gospel as a lifestyle, naturally, takes a lifetime. We're not putting on a show or a presentation, we're not aggressively targeting people as projects—this is real life, and we're dealing with real souls. What a joy to do the work of the Lord and to see the Lord work in and through us to change lives. Never let it grow old. Never lose hope. Keep learning, keep growing, keep sharing. We have a faith so real, so powerful, and so solid that we can't help but spread it with joy.

PERSONAL (OR GROUP) QUESTIONS

1. Have you ever shared the Gospel? Describe your experience(s).
2. What are some of the apologetics questions that you have heard around you that would be helpful to study up on?
3. Have you ever had questions about your faith? How did you work through them? What answers did you find?

Today's Challenge

Learn a few apologetics answers to some common faith questions—the existence of God, the intelligent design of creation, the resurrection of Jesus, and so forth. Many great resources are available to help you learn more, such as answersingenesis.org and their Answers books, movies by Living Waters (livingwaters.com), and *The Case for Christ* by Lee Strobel.

DAY 11

Ministry

Then I heard the voice of the Lord, saying, "Whom shall I send,
and who will go for Us?" Then I said, "Here am I. Send me!"
ISAIAH 6:8

People everywhere are looking for freedom from their guilt, shame, and problems. Answering these seekers are many voices out in the world offering false hope. We Christians bear the world's best-kept secret—the Gospel. While many people have at least heard of Jesus, we'd be shocked to realize how many people don't even know the Gospel story, much less understand what Jesus did for them, what implications His sacrifice has for their lives, and what the Bible teaches. People are searching for truth—the truth that sets us free (John 8:32)! We just cannot keep the good news to ourselves.

Once we have Jesus, our life becomes one big mission trip. This planet is our mission field—starting right in our hometown, perhaps venturing beyond. There are so many different people, places, backgrounds, problems, needs. . . . Where do we begin? First, we need to realize something about those unique talents, skills, circumstances, positions, opportunities, and stories that shape our lives— God has very intentionally prepared us for His calling on our lives so that we can bring Him glory.

That is why we share our faith, after all: to glorify God and point others to the Lord. For the unsaved, we point them to salvation in Jesus. For believers, we help them grow and draw closer to Him. We share what God has taught us in our lives and from the scriptures. We help them draw closer and closer to Jesus. All the while, our faith is being strengthened. God uses our active obedience in shining His light to the world as a means for us to grow, stretch, and ultimately draw closer to Him.

As we humbly bring what God has given us and blessed us with to the table and selflessly give it back to Him, He is glorified. It's not about us. It's about God first and others next. It's not about bringing us glory, fame, a good name, praise, whatever—our desire and motivation ought to be purely to bring glory to the holy name of God. He is deserving of every bit of our devoted worship, honor, and praise (Psalm 145:21). We call this ministry—we minister to others to help them, point them to Christ, and bring glory to God. Ministry isn't just for professionals with ThDs—it's for everyone who calls Jesus Lord. It's for you and me.

So now we may have some questions: *What is God calling me to do? How do I do it? What is my ministry?* All excellent questions. While God may have multiple callings on our lives, our ultimate calling is proclaiming His name, His Gospel, and bringing Him glory. I believe that sharing the Gospel, encouraging fellow believers, and living as a godly example to other believers (1 Timothy 4:12) should be a lifestyle, not an activity. I also believe our first ministry priority is our family—right now with our parents and siblings, and someday as wives and moms. God also has many creative ministry opportunities that He's chosen specifically for us, whether they be short or long term.

Ministry can look like anything from singing at nursing homes to taking part in mission trips to blogging to having a conversation with someone at the coffee shop. It can be mentoring a younger girl or serving at church. It can be raising money for an organization or volunteering your time or services. It can be creating artwork or writing letters or articles or taking advantage of a platform God has given us to make a difference for His kingdom. I don't know what God has for your ministry at this point in your life, but I know He often places burdens on our hearts that are in sync with His mission for us. Here are some things we can think about in determining His work for us right now:

- *Has God put a specific demographic or place on your heart?* Some people feel a strong call to overseas missions—maybe even to a specific country or people group. Some have been given a heart and a knack for caring for children. Maybe you feel called to influence girls your age or younger. Maybe you want to reach out to single mothers, widows, and orphans. Who do you feel God calling you to minister to?

- *Has God placed a burden on your heart for a specific cause?* It's that heavy feeling we get in our hearts and in the pits of our stomachs—a yearning or even a sickening ache. We burn with righteous anger when we hear about the injustice of human trafficking. We passionately desire to help families who are crumbling. We long to help the many children waiting in foster care. We desperately wish to encourage girls to stay pure and wait for their future husbands.

Sometimes God uses our own testimonies to ignite our passion—maybe we've had struggles in our lives and overcome them by the power of the Holy Spirit, and now God wants us to help and encourage other girls with the same struggles. Our background and personal experience give us an even stronger voice behind our message. Someone who has experienced her parents' divorce can relate to and help another girl in the same situation in a way that others could not. Someone who has struggled with an eating disorder can give advice to another girl with the same struggle, and her testimony can be an encouragement to her that there is hope for freedom. See what I mean? God is so good and so creative. He can use any situation or past experience for good and for His glory (Romans 8:28).

- *What are your God-given passions and talents?* Maybe you're an amazing speaker or a talented artist. Maybe ballet or music is your thing. Maybe you're a bold debater or a poetic songwriter. Maybe you like cinematography, graphic design, the medical field, history, the culinary arts, sports, math and science, who knows! Each of us is brimming with special talents and unique qualities that make us one-of-a-kind assets for God's great work.

Determine what you can do right now to make God's name known and proclaim the truth of His Word—then put wheels beneath it. Pray for God to show you when, where, and how to do it. Ask Him to provide the means and open up opportunities to accomplish His work—and ultimately to bring His name glory through you. He longs to use us if only we will ask and make ourselves available! We have to submit with reverent obedience to our loving Lord.

God's ministry adventures for me in the past few years have included writing *The Greatest Book You've Never Read* in 2013, speaking and leading worship at a girls' conference put on by a local ministry, professionally recording the cover song "Wonderful Merciful Savior" with my sister in January 2016, and landing a publishing deal for this book. What a beautiful, humbling experience to witness God's faithfulness in taking someone as imperfect as me and opening doors to make a difference for others. He's done it for me, and I guarantee you He wants to do it for you. Just keep your eyes peeled—His ministry opportunities come in all kinds of packages.

Remember the real focus—why we share our faith in the first place. It's all too easy to lose sight of why we're doing what we're doing. One look around us and we can get proud, overconfident, and independent of God, forgetting that God is the only reason we are even able to make a difference. We must have a healthy estimation of our weaknesses and our inadequacy without Him, acknowledging that He is the One who makes us capable, strong, and sufficient. It's all about pointing others to Him and bringing all the glory to the holy, mighty name of Jesus—because He truly deserves our all.

PERSONAL (OR GROUP) QUESTIONS

1. Name a couple of your talents and skills. Now name some people (in your life or in scripture) who have used these same or similar talents for the glory of God.

2. What are some of the passions and burdens God has placed on your heart, possibly for ministry?

3. What are some of the "mission fields"—places where you can minister to others—in your day-to-day life?

Today's Challenge
Brainstorm ways you can use your God-given assets to minister to others. Ask God who He wants you to minister to and how.

THEN I heard THE voice OF THE Lord saying, "WHOM shall I SEND? AND who will go for US?" Then I said, "HERE am I SEND me!" ISAIAH 6:8

Standing Up for What's Right

Therefore do not be ashamed of the testimony of our Lord or of me His prisoner,
but join with me in suffering for the gospel according to the power of God.
2 Timothy 1:8

If you've never read *The Insanity of God* by Nik Ripken, then I need you to grab your reading list (you *do* have a reading list, right?) and add that title as the very next book you're going to read. It's incredibly hard not to be moved by this contemporary missionary's journey researching the persecuted church around the globe. For me, it was a powerful perspective changer: in my southern neck of the USA, I can't imagine the hardships that come with being a believer in a communist country where church happens in secret. It's hard for me to grasp the thought of being imprisoned for my faith—yet this book highlights the stories of many individuals all over the world who had a bold, relentless faith that they would not deny. They would not keep to themselves what Jesus had done for the world. They carried the Gospel faithfully—even at the cost of their lives.

One of my favorite moments in the book is when the author, Nik Ripken, hears the story of an older man who has faithfully suffered harsh persecution in his lifetime for the sake of the Gospel. Ripken writes, "Then he raised his voice in a prophet-like challenge that I knew would live with me forever: 'Don't ever give up in freedom what we would never have given up in persecution! That is our witness to the power of the resurrection of Jesus Christ!' "* That statement greatly convicted me. Some of my fellow brothers and sisters in Christ have been through it all and yet still shamelessly proclaim the name of Jesus. How often do we cop out of sharing the Gospel with the people around us, or shrink from speaking the truth? How easy it is to falter when everyone else is doing wrong, even though we know what is right.

What keeps us from declaring the Gospel in our own corner of this great big mission field? It's fear. Fear of suffering: In my country, people might dismiss you or think you're strange. It might feel awkward. Someone might ask you to please stop. You might even get labeled intolerant or, worse, a *hater*. But across the ocean? It's common to be imprisoned for years at a time. Families are separated. There's physical and psychological torture. In some places, being a Christian means being willing to give up *everything*—including your own life. When I hear these true persecution accounts, I feel remorse for my apathy, and I realize that what we have here doesn't compare to the persecution on a global scale. We have complete freedom to share the Gospel that brings light into the darkness—yet why does it seem that the Great Commission to share this Gospel is being fulfilled more obediently in places where there is great hostility? The underground churches seem to understand "church" better than we do.

The question is, will you and I faithfully obey Christ even when it will cost us something? Not too often does the Gospel demand our physical life in the United States, but our lives are indeed in question. Will we surrender our entire selves to the God we made our Lord? Will we share about the life-changing love of Jesus or keep it to ourselves? Will we say no to compromise, yes to standards, and yes to the scriptures? Will we stand up for the truth and for what's right even when we're standing alone? Jesus warned us that if we follow Him, the world will hate us because it hated Him first! It will disown us, because we are not its own! The world doesn't have a problem with us believers ourselves—they have a problem with the One we believe in and are proclaiming (John 15:18–21).

Someone devoted to Christ and His truth will feel lonely at times. Being the only one to make biblical choices, to live a God-centered life, and to openly talk about it can feel strange. You and I get this—it feels awkward to be different! But when we're different, standing alone and letting our devotion to our Lord and King be stronger than the ruling of our internal social awkwardness gauge, people take notice.

It starts with the little things—those choices we make because we love the

Lord and desire to glorify Him through a pure and holy living testimony. People will ask questions, of course, because they're curious to know: Why *don't* you watch those kinds of movies or listen to those kinds of songs? Why do you give *your* money to your church? Why do you help that person out when you know he or she won't pay you back? Why does it matter what we believe? Why do you care about dressing modestly? What's the big deal about purity? Why don't you cuss? What makes you so joyful?

People see the difference Jesus makes in our lives. Of course we still make mistakes sometimes. We're nowhere near perfect. We're still human—still learning, still growing, still seeking the Lord about the choices we should be making. But faithfulness to stick to God's Word and to our convictions based on what He has revealed to us through His Word—as best as we understand it and apply it—will glorify the Lord and equip us to stand strong through whatever circumstances come our way.

But how can we possibly stand alone? How can we do it without the world breaking us? How can we bear the mockery, the shunning, the hatred? How can we cope with the darkness and the loneliness? The answer is simple but has *huge* implications: Jesus! We are *never* alone if we are constantly abiding in the presence of our Lord. He is always with us. And He has fully overcome the world (John 16:33). Yes, the darkness and the enemy are bigger than us in our own strength, but the One living inside of us is even *bigger* than them: "You are from God, little children, and have overcome them; because greater is He who is in you than he who is in the world" (1 John 4:4).

Jesus helps us to stand strong when we feel we can no longer take the fire; He is our strength (Isaiah 40:29). He lets us spill our worries, cares, and fears before His throne, and He takes our loads (1 Peter 5:7). He gives us His everlasting words to cling to, like Matthew 11:30, Romans 5:3–5, 1 Corinthians 10:13, and 1 Peter 5:9. He teaches us to depend on Him alone and to desire His approval above anyone else's. Second Corinthians 4:16–18 describes our hope—the light at the end of the tunnel—as we fix our eyes on what will last forever.

God did not make us to walk through life alone, though. When we feel the need to stand alone is often when we need to stand together the most. We need fellowship with the body of Christ—with the church. As believers, we can support one another, battling darkness on the same side as joint forces of light. We must be in unity, continually refreshed by the hospitality of other like-minded, Bible-grounded believers.

Please pray for me and your other sisters and brothers in Christ. I'll pray for you. Pray for the Christ followers around the world who face persecution daily. Pray that they will choose to continue in their boldness for the Gospel, in their love for Jesus and others, and in their daily reliance upon God. We have a faith worth living and dying for.

PERSONAL (OR GROUP) QUESTIONS

1. When was a time you experienced a level of persecution for your faith?
2. What are some ways you can stand strong when standing alone?
3. Who are people in your life or in the Bible who inspire you to stand up for what is right? What qualities do they possess?

Today's Challenge

Pray for the endurance and boldness of those in the persecuted church. Visit persecution.com for specific prayer requests of Christians in oppressed countries.

---

*Nik Ripken with Gregg Lewis, *The Insanity of God: A True Story of Faith Resurrected* (Nashville: B&H, 2013), 196.

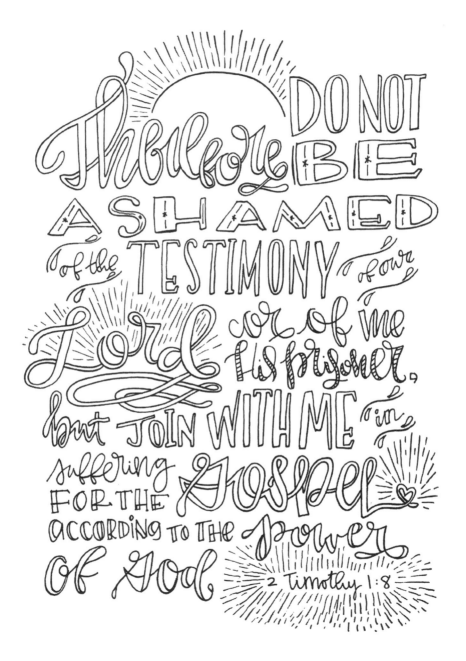

Therefore DO NOT BE ASHAMED of the TESTIMONY of our Lord or of me his prisoner, but JOIN WITH ME in suffering FOR THE GOSPEL according to the power of God

2 Timothy 1:8

Fearlessness

*"Do not fear, for I am with you; do not anxiously look about you,
for I am your God. I will strengthen you, surely I will help you,
surely I will uphold you with My righteous right hand."*
Isaiah 41:10

Fear—it's paralyzing and suffocating. It disarms us of our fight and leaves us frozen in our tracks. One wrong move and we'll be punished for it. What's even scarier is that some of us live in fear every single day. With hearts full of dread and terror, we hardly have the capacity to recognize that this is not the quality of life God intended us to have.

When I got into my later teens and had to start making some big decisions about life ahead of me, I became anxious and didn't take my worries to God and seek Him at first. *What if He doesn't answer me? What if I don't hear Him correctly? What if I make the wrong decision and virtually ruin my future?* Fear is great at taking our issues and blowing them out of proportion so they grow too big for us to carry or handle. I feared the future, what might be ahead, and assumed the responsibility of that burden upon my own back. Praise the Lord, I've continually been learning how to listen to the voice of the Lord. God has guided me through stressful and high-pressure decision making. But I also realized the power I had given fear in my life. I had let it take over my ability to reason and think straight when things were crazy.

What is there to be afraid of? There are plenty of phobias: public speaking, death, losing a loved one, rejection, harm, pain, illness, humiliation, spiders. . .(shudder). The list goes on and on. Some are funny or irrational, but others are serious and make a whole lot of sense. Who wouldn't be afraid of something that has the power to change their whole life for the worse—like death? It's real, grim, and powerful. Sometimes fear is rooted in reality. We have no control over the winds of change and circumstance, and we dread the thought of being their prey.

Fear is *not* from God. Rather, it is a trap to keep us from fully trusting and obeying God's great plans for us. If fear keeps us glued in our tracks, then the enemy has no concern that we're going to get in the way of his evil plans. But you know what is from God? Power, love, and a sound mind (2 Timothy 1:7 NKJV). You see, we're not helpless victims at the mercy of our fears. We can choose to let fear—or Jesus—take control.

We have to choose to put our faith in God. Sometimes we look at the waves around us and see their power as they roll and surge, threatening to capsize us (Matthew 14:30). It's true—many of our fears are valid and powerful. But we must not take our eyes off Jesus, who is standing right there, the One in control of the wind and the waves. Our God has more power than anything we fear. He has more power than darkness, than Satan himself. He is in control of our world, and He has a detailed plan for our lives. Death can't come any sooner than He will let it. Hardships have only as much impact as He will allow—and He works all things together for good in the end (Romans 8:28). He grows us and makes us more like Christ, if we let Him. The fact that God holds me in the palm of His hand, that He is in control of the craziness around me, and that He has a beautifully mapped out plan for my life is incredibly assuring to me.

Fear has no place in the life of someone who fears the Lord. Fear of the Lord is a worshipful respect—we take the Lord seriously and revere the One who holds the power of life and death. If we don't fear Him, then what can stop us from forever living in our fears? Fear of the Lord is quite a different kind of fear, really; we aren't terrified of approaching Him, but rather we live with a holy dread of His powerful judgments, while at the same time loving Him with our whole hearts and knowing His deep love and goodness toward us. Matthew 10:28 deflects us from worldly fear to the fear of the Lord: "Do not fear those who kill the body but are unable to kill the soul; but rather fear Him who is able to destroy both soul and body in hell." Our motivation to obey the good Lord whom we love, whom we respect and serve, and who has good plans for us ought to prevail over the fears and worries we have.

So what are we going to do about fear? We won't let fear rule our lives and ruin everything as it keeps us from moving, speaking, living, breathing, and loving. No longer will we let fear choke us! But how do we overcome it? Even just the thought of dealing with fear can be scary. But here's the key to triumphing over fear: *love*—God's perfect love. First John 4:18 makes a healing claim: "There is no fear in love; but perfect love casts out fear, because fear involves punishment, and the one who fears is not perfected in love."

When we have 100 percent confidence that we are completely loved by our good Father, we have not a single reason to fear. What's the worst that can happen? We're safely nestled in the fullest love in existence, found in the most trustworthy heart of our Lord. We can be brave, regardless of the hardships we may experience during our days on earth. We have put our undivided confidence and faith in the God of the universe, and He never, ever fails us. Psalm 56:11 says, "In God I have put my trust, I shall not be afraid. What can man do to me?"

Bravery doesn't mean we never feel scared. Our feelings may toss, turn, and churn right along with the waves around us, but we can stand firm on the solid truths found in God's Word. We can choose to let fear lose as we trust in God and move forward in obedience to Him, despite quaking knees or chattering teeth. Our deep confidence in God's ability and sovereignty will fuel our own confidence that we "can do all things through Him who strengthens [us]" (Philippians 4:13). God is calling us to some amazing adventures—and He will be with us every step of the way. In Him, we are fearless.

1. What do you fear? Do these fears ever hinder you from trusting the Lord? How?

2. Think of someone who exemplifies bravery, either in your life or in God's Word. What lessons can you learn from that person's fearlessness?

3. What are some ways you can conquer the fears you mentioned? What are God's promises to you?

Today's Challenge

Write your fears on a piece of toilet paper—you know where this is going. That's right, flush it down the toilet. Release your worries and fears to the Lord, and thank Him for His perfect love, protection, and care for you.

DO NOT FEAR

FOR I AM WITH YOU;

do not ANXIOUSLY LOOK about you,

FOR I AM YOUR GOD.

I WILL STRENGTHEN YOU

SURELY I WILL UPHOLD YOU

w/ MY RIGHTEOUS RIGHT HAND.

ISAIAH 41:10

Forgiveness

*Be kind to one another, tender-hearted, forgiving each other,
just as God in Christ also has forgiven you.*
EPHESIANS 4:32

Forgive them? After what they did to me? After what they said? After how much it all hurt? Forgiveness can be a tall order. Wounds inflicted intentionally or even unintentionally can cut deep and hurt badly. Offenses can breach the best of relationships, ruin the fondest of memories, and overpower the kindest of words spoken in the past. Mistakes can mar a relationship for a long time and even for life sometimes. And yet God tells us to *forgive?*

I don't know what you're harboring in your heart right now. Some of us struggle to forgive the friend who didn't keep her word. The person who made a thoughtless remark on a bad day. The road-raging driver who cut us off. The constant complainer. The miscommunicator. The nosy busybody. The girl who gossips so much it's quite possible she works for a tabloid. The person whose rejection of us has broken our heart and left us in tears. A family member we skirmished with. You name the issue, offenses—little or big—can irk, annoy, anger, sadden, and embitter our hearts.

Offense, without interference, morphs into bitterness—a painful resentment that leaves us not only wallowing in self-pity, but also feeling angry with the guilty party. A strong grudge develops and a defensive wall goes up. *They don't deserve my forgiveness. They had no right to do what they did. I have every right to keep this grudge.* Have any of these thoughts ever gone through your head? I know they've gone through mine. Sure, there are times when I contribute to a problem, but there are other times when I am innocent and the other party involved is clearly in the wrong—those are the times I feel I have a legitimate right to with-hold my forgiveness.

Problem is, holding a grudge and growing bitter is like drinking poison and hoping it hurts the other person. In other words, the only people we're hurting are ourselves! Rather than addressing the hurt, forgiving the offender, and allowing the wound to heal, we harden our hearts because we've been in a vulnerable state, experiencing pain, and we just don't want to put ourselves back in that place. Friends, I'm not preaching here; I struggle with holding grudges just like you. *Our response makes sense.*

Yet in the midst of "sense," God's Word is truth. Ephesians 4:32 gives us an impossible task: "Be kind to one another, tender-hearted, forgiving each other, just as God in Christ also has forgiven you." Thankfully, our God is the God of the impossible. With some offenses, forgiveness is simply impossible to dole out on our own. That's why we shouldn't even try to forgive without God's help—because nothing is impossible with Him (Mark 10:27).

Here is the key to forgiveness: *remember.* Remember how we were forgiven. God had every reason—every *right*—to leave our human race wallowing in our sins after we turned our hearts away from Him, and ultimately to just let us burn in hell. But His love was far greater, and He not only extends His forgiveness freely but actually gave His life for us *while we were still sinners* (Romans 5:8). Think about your own sins that He has forgiven, forgotten, and thrown "as far as the east is from the west" (Psalm 103:12). I think about all the sins I've commit-ted against Him and against others, and I'm blown away that He not only has forgiven me, redeemed me, and cleansed me but also calls me pure, holy, loved, justified, chosen, *His*! I am God's daughter! His forgiveness capacity is unfathom-ably huge. You and I have been forgiven of so much. How can we not extend the same forgiveness to others, from one imperfect person to another? With forgive-ness like we've received, we simply *have* to (Matthew 6:14–15). We have a perfect God who has set the perfect example.

So forgive—the misdemeanors and the major offenses, the family, the friends, the coworkers, the angry drivers, the bullies. Even forgive yourself—yes, we are so undeserving of God's forgiveness, yet out of His vast love for us, He lavishes it on us anyway! In Christ we are no longer guilty. First John 1:9 tells us, "If we confess our sins, He is faithful and righteous to forgive us our sins and to cleanse us from all unrighteousness." We are clean and pure once again. Jesus in our hearts washes us clean.

I am aware that some of the seemingly "big" offenses I've dealt with in my life are not the only kinds of things people struggle to forgive. Some have received much deeper wounds: abuse, misuse, neglect, rejection, trauma, and life-altering tragedy. Offenses like these are not easily forgotten, recovered from, or put right— but to *forgive*? Is that even fair to ask—even possible?

Meet my friend Corrie ten Boom. I would have loved to meet this godly hero of mine—a single Dutch clockmaker who hid Jews during World War II and ended up getting caught and sent to a concentration camp. By the sheer grace of God in a complete miracle situation, she survived and was released years later—but not without scars in her life. Her sister Betsie had died in the camp. She had witnessed some of the most gruesome and hateful torture and killing that ever took place in history. She was treated like an animal—worse, actually. After all she went through, she had every right to be bitter. Every right to hate those people who had hated her first. Every reason to hate life, to despise human- ity, and to give up trust. She even could've chosen to blame God.

Corrie's story, however, does not end with a hardened heart encased in that poison called bitterness. Despite her awful situation and her every reason to carry a burdensome grudge upon her back, she chose to *forgive*. She forgave the people who ran the atrocious torture camps. She even forgave the guard whom she witnessed beating weak Betsie. Ultimately, the Lord used Corrie's story to impact lives all over the world as she spoke about her experiences and God's goodness. I can't do her story justice; read it for yourself in her book *The Hiding Place*.

How was Corrie able to extend forgiveness? She realized something: if she was going to forgive all the horrendous wrongs she'd experienced, she was going to need every bit of the Lord's help and love deposited in her heart—*regardless* of her feelings. "Forgiveness is an act of the will," Corrie said, "and the will can function regardless of the temperature of the heart."* Feelings may follow later, but "do not grow weary of doing good" (2 Thessalonians 3:13). Let's make the choice to forgive—and be set free.

PERSONAL (OR GROUP) QUESTIONS

1. What do you find the hardest about extending forgiveness? What about receiving forgiveness?

2. How does the knowledge of God's forgiveness of your sins affect your heart toward others?

3. What is your response when it comes to forgiving yourself? Have you held any personal grudges that you need to release before the Lord?

Today's Challenge

Ask the Holy Spirit to bring to mind anyone with whom you need to make things right. He gives us strength to do what's right, even when we feel weak.

---

*Corrie ten Boom, *Tramp for the Lord* (Berkley: Jove Books, 1978), 55.

True Beauty

"O my love, you are altogether beautiful and fair.
There is no flaw nor blemish in you!"
Song of Solomon 4:7 AMP

What a smashingly beautiful world we live in. No one can walk outside after a heavy thunderstorm, watch the sun rise through the dramatic fog of early morning, or step into the vast blue ocean lapping against the sandy coast and think God doesn't care about beauty. Clearly, God has an eye for design. But the beautiful hardly stops at nature—God made us in His image, and He is the epitome of beautiful (Revelation 1:13–15). Beauty is meant to reflect God's glory and splendor. He created us to behold, enjoy, and exhibit His beauty.

Woven into the fabric that makes us women is the desire to be beautiful, and when anyone—even ourselves—tells us that we are otherwise, we struggle with feeling unhappy, inferior, and unacceptable. We can become so focused on outward appearance that we lose sight of God's idea of beautiful—especially when our clothes aren't fitting quite right, we despise our unphotogenic smile, and we look nothing like the Photoshopped models we're told we should resemble. The media's philosophy? Either you're "hot," or you're just *not*.

But my question is: *Who are they to say who's beautiful and who's not?* Do they have the right to set the standard for beauty because they themselves are "10s"? For that matter, who determines who's a "10"? Truth is, the path to becoming that kind of "beautiful" is just an empty, unfulfilling, painful road of compromise and broken dreams—it's an ugly lie. The chase isn't worth it; after all, physical beauty won't last forever (Proverbs 31:30). That kind of competitive, seductive, unreachable beauty doesn't reflect the Creator's glory; it just leaves us dissatisfied, because guess what—there's always someone more and someone less pretty. It's a game we'll never win.

So many girls go crazy believing ugly lies. There are physically gorgeous girls who can't stand the way they look. Unhealthily skinny girls who genuinely think they need to lose weight. Pretty girls who don't bother taking care of themselves because they don't think they're worth it.

If only they would believe the truth—God's definition of beautiful. First Peter 3:3–4 says, "Your adornment must not be merely external—braiding the hair, and wearing gold jewelry, or putting on dresses; but let it be the hidden person of the heart, with the imperishable quality of a gentle and quiet spirit, which is precious in the sight of God." And we must not forget Proverbs 31:30 (NLT), for it starts with, "Charm is deceptive, and beauty does not last," but concludes with, "but a woman who fears the LORD will be greatly praised."

All right, straight from God's Word, here's the truth about it all: Outward beauty is nice, but it isn't everything! It's not as valuable as the condition of our hearts. It will eventually fade, but real beauty found on the inside will not. A girl who is devoted to serving Jesus desires to make her heart a beautiful dwelling place for her King. Underneath the exterior of her appearance lies this priceless deposit of beauty within. It's who we are, not just what we look like, that makes us beautiful.

What is this "gentle and quiet spirit" that God finds so valuable? A wild, restless spirit revels in opposing and rebelling against God to chase her own fleshly whims, but a gentle and quiet spirit trusts the Lord, submits to His will, follows Him wholeheartedly, and deeply desires to please Him. Her life and obedience are expressions of her loyalty and love for the Lord.

And finally, "a woman who fears the LORD will be greatly praised"—a reverent fear of the Lord is worth far more than beautiful looks in the grand scheme of things. Fear of the Lord is what will keep us from sin; to fear Him means to take Him seriously. He doesn't trifle about sin and about His commandments. To protect us and lead us into His perfect plan for our lives, He requires our submission, obedience, and devotion. "The fear of the LORD is to hate evil," Proverbs 8:13 says.

Fear of the Lord survives well past the prime of beauty into wrinkles and gray hair.

This kind of beautiful is full of worth, fulfillment, and joy. It is purposeful and selfless. Its ultimate end is to bring glory to God. I want to be that kind of beautiful girl—not so hung up on my outward appearance that I miss out on serving Jesus and celebrating the golden beauty of a heart that is completely in love with Him. I want to believe when I hear my Lord say, "O my love, you are altogether beautiful and fair. There is no flaw nor blemish in you!" (Song of Solomon 4:7 AMP). I want to love the way God made me and thank Him for it. See, it's not that we should disregard the way we look, but rather we ought to make our heart and life all about reflecting Jesus. That, my friends, is true beauty.

Here's a thought on those temporary tents we call our physical bodies: they are also the temples of the Holy Spirit if Jesus is dwelling in our hearts (1 Corinthians 6:19). We don't get to choose the physical appearance we are born with, but we certainly can do something with what we've been given. I believe God has given every girl outward beauty—it's all about making the most of what we've got! If I may offer a few tips:

- *Smile more!* Laughter and joy happen to be two very attractive (and contagious) qualities; a glowing, genuine smile will do wonders for our appearance. While I'm at it, I would recommend against the duck face. Please. Smiling is way prettier—trust me on that one.
- *Take proper care of yourself.* Maintain cleanliness and good hygiene, keeping your hair, nails, and teeth healthy and clean right along with the rest of your body. (Quick beauty tip: swish—don't swallow!—a capful of hydrogen peroxide in your mouth for a couple of seconds, spit, and brush for a whiter set of teeth!) Exercise regularly and eat moderate portions of the right foods. Taking good care of the bodies God has given us not only is good stewardship but will improve our overall appearance.
- *Enhance, don't distract.* We can wear modest, fashionable clothing in a way that glorifies God, draws attention to our face and who we are, and gives our appearance a boost. We can use makeup to enhance our natural features, not to cake over the things we don't like or to change the way we look—that's what

clowns do. We can style our hair—or brush it at least.

Beauty—inside, outside, and upside down—is a gift from God and a reflection of His glory. The only conclusion left to draw, then, is that our outward beauty should be a reflection of the beautiful work God is doing inside our hearts. What is more beautiful than the Lord patiently refining imperfect people like us into brilliant diamonds as He purifies us and shapes us to be more and more like Jesus every single day? He makes us beautiful.

PERSONAL (OR GROUP) QUESTIONS

1. What are some lies you have believed about beauty—maybe about yourself? What is God's truth about those lies?

2. What is one beautiful character quality you possess? What is one you can work on this week?

3. What are some ways you can reflect the Lord's beauty within you through your outward appearance?

Today's Challenge

Thank God for the flawlessly beautiful way He made you, inside and out. Ask Him to bring to mind someone you can affirm today about her true God-given beauty.

My love, you are altogether beautiful & fair. There is no flaw or blemish in you.

Song of Solomon 4:7

DAY 16

True Love

The one who does not love does not know God, for God is love.
1 JOHN 4:8

Let's talk about love—*true love*. Quite possibly the most beautiful, most power-ful, most amazing, most confusing, most misapplied, most overused words ever spoken. We've witnessed our fair share of fiery romances, whether in a Hall-mark Christmas movie, a little house on a prairie, or a *Peanuts* comic strip. But romance—as romantic as it may be—is not even half of true love. *Eros*, the Greek word for romantic love, is only one of four types of love. There's also *storge*, the family bond; *philia*, a friendship connection; and *agape*, unconditional love.

I'm not sure anything in life is better than loving and being loved. Yet look around—"love" is a mess! A skyrocketing divorce rate, family members who virtually hate each other's guts, friendships unfriended into enemy status, and. . .unconditional love? Oh please, there are always strings attached. Whether in marriage or any other relationship, love is most often seen as a contract: I keep my side of the deal to be there for your needs *only* if you keep your side of the deal to be there for my needs. If not, see ya—I'm outta here.

It's sad but startlingly true. And we're left wondering, is true love even *the truth*? Is it even a real thing? We've taken mental note of the many examples of selfish love—if we can even call it love—all around us, but the perfect example of true love is right under our noses—in our hearts, actually.

You and I are loved with a love "as strong as death," with a "jealousy un-yielding as the grave. It burns like blazing fire, like a mighty flame. Many waters cannot quench love; rivers cannot sweep it away" (Song of Solomon 8:6–7 NIV). That's God's love for us. Never let God's love become cliché or tainted by the false kinds of love you've seen, because His love is beyond anything we've ever experienced.

His love is pure and passionate. His love accepts us the way we are—with our good, our bad, our past, our sins, and our flaws all bare before His loving eyes—and He loves us enough not to let us stay that way. He washes us, changes us, teaches us, and grows us, but not in a harsh, abrasive, angry way. Rather, He is the absolute perfect Father, a complete gentleman, kind and tender, reminding us of our worth and beauty as His daughters. He has great, ambitious, wild plans for our lives and wants to hold our hands every step of the way. He wants to pick us up when we fall, and He forgives and blesses us generously. He has a good heart that loves unconditionally. He loves us with agape love.

Isn't it wonderful to be loved with such ardor and purpose? There's good news: His love never fails (1 Corinthians 13:8). Want to hear some more good news? We can love like that, too. Not in our own human strength or willpower, of course, but by the Holy Spirit perfecting God's love in our hearts (1 John 4:12). See, the more we get to know God, grow close to Him, and abide in His sweet, loving presence, the more we will love others. It's just the way love works: the deeper we know God's love for us and for others, the more we can't help but love others as an act of loving obedience to God.

First John 4:20 tells it like it is: "If someone says, 'I love God,' and hates his brother, he is a liar; for the one who does not love his brother whom he has seen, cannot love God whom he has not seen." Of course. How can we directly defy God's command to love the ones He has placed in our lives and *still* say that we love Him? Our good works and obedience to God's Word do not come from the motivation to earn salvation (which is a free gift!), but rather from our love and reverence for the Lord, who gave us His all so we could keep on giving and loving like He has done for us.

To love others to the fullest capacity, we must love God first and most. Someday I hope to be an adoring, devoted wife. I will never be able to love my future husband to the fullest if I don't love God more and put Him first. I can't be a kind, patient sister and respectful, honoring daughter if I don't love the Lord first and most. I will be a B-quality friend if I neglect my relationship with the Lord and don't put Him first in my life. And I will certainly attach conditions to my loving treatment of others, because without a solid reason to love others fully and unconditionally, I'll just be led by my emotions (which are crazy, by the way).

But as we grow in our love for God and in our knowledge of His love, we begin to change. We see others differently. No longer is that annoying, attention-hungry girl at school an object of our spite, but rather we see a girl longing for love. A girl whom God loves enormously, yet she doesn't get it. A girl whom God may want to reach through our love.

But don't expect the quest to love others to be all easy and breezy. As we learn more about true love, we realize it is less butterflies and glittery eyes. In reality, true love happens when the stars don't align, sparks dim, and butterflies have flown away. True love happens when we know we will get nothing in return. We give and they take. True love is a sacrifice. We are patient, kind, never envious, never boastful—we model 1 Corinthians 13 in our hearts and with our behavior without expecting payback or accolade. We lay down our lives for others—maybe for people we don't like very much or even people who hate us. Maybe for people we have every reason to despise because of what they've done. But we remember why we love.

God *so* loved us while we were still sinners (Romans 5:8), still God-hating evildoers. And God *so* loved us that He sent Jesus to die for us. John 3:16—the first verse a church kid ever memorizes, but also one of the most powerful reminders of what love really means. We've all battled with the thought, *Why am I doing this? Why should I keep on loving this person when it's so ridiculously hard?* We know the answer because we know God's love. *God so loves this person. They are magnificently precious in His eyes. He thinks this person is worth dying for. He died for me and loves me.*

First John 4:8 says, "The one who does not love does not know God, for God is love." I hope you find true love. I hope you and I grow so close to God that we naturally begin to "love from a pure heart and a good conscience and a sincere faith" (1 Timothy 1:5). May we model 1 Peter 1:22: "Since you have in obedience to the truth purified your souls for a sincere love of the brethren, fervently love one another from the heart." May you and I, whether we be sisters, daughters, friends, students, coworkers, acquaintances, or even wives and mothers someday, so overflow with God's love that it runs up and over onto everyone we meet. His love will never fail, because God Himself is true love, and God never fails.

PERSONAL (OR GROUP) QUESTIONS

1. What are some ways you have shown Christ's love? What 1 Corinthians 13 love qualities do you need to work on? What goals can you set in these areas?
2. What aspects or qualities of God's love stand out to you personally?
3. What examples of true, unconditional, agape love have you witnessed in your life?

Today's Challenge

Write out each of the 1 Corinthians 13 love qualities: patience, kindness, and so forth. Pray that the Lord would help you cultivate each character trait in your day-to-day interactions with people you love, like, and don't like. May His love reign in your heart.

LOVE

The one who does not love does not know God, for God is

first john 4:8

True Purity

Create in me a pure heart, O God.
PSALM 51:10 NIV

If there's one topic every Christian girls' author has addressed, it's purity. Everyone has *something* to say, be it right or wrong, loose or conservative, broad or specific. While plenty of "two cents" have been invested in the subject, purity is a seriously important element of our walk with God. And not only is it a crucial topic, but it is one that much of the Christian world is getting wrong.

Christian guys and girls are pros at talking the talk and getting on mission trip and youth conference "highs for Jesus," but when it comes down to making right choices, standing blameless before God, and keeping heart, body, mind, soul, and spirit pure, humble, and full of the fear of the Lord—there's a disconnect. Purity is not a ring, a book, or even a commitment, though all of those can be good things! But without the active maintaining of our whole selves according to God's Word (Psalm 119:9), they are only symbols and "good Christian girl" clichés.

Often we limit the purity discussion to talk about staying pure in guy-girl relationships, saving ourselves for the future husband God has for us, and that kind of thing. Yes, there is that angle of it, but purity goes way deeper than just romantic relationships. Purity happens when Jesus in our lives begins to change us and remove the gross filth from our hearts, minds, souls, and spirits. He *sanctifies* us, meaning He washes us in His truth and in His cleansing, healing blood.

Physical purity is just a start—but it's one worth starting at! When we realize whose we are (God's), it changes the way we view, carry, treat, and represent our bodies. When God made us, He modeled us after Himself: "God created man in His own image" (Genesis 1:27). As Christians, we have the Holy Spirit of God Himself dwelling within us—our bodies are His temple! First Corinthians 6:19–20 tells it plainly: "Do you not know that your body is a temple of the Holy Spirit who is in you, whom you have from God, and that you are not your own? For you have been bought with a price: therefore glorify God in your body." We were made to glorify God with everything we have—including our physical bodies. "The body is not for immorality, but for the Lord, and the Lord is for the body" (1 Corinthians 6:13).

Purity, in its literal sense, is freedom from contamination. Water is pure if it is completely clean. What about our hearts? Our minds? It is possible for someone to be pure on the outside but filthy on the inside. Sins committed in the quiet secrecy of our hearts and minds are *still sins to God*. In Matthew 5:27–29, Jesus made it clear that lust—occurring only in the heart and mind, where nobody else can see it—is still a sin. God isn't just evaluating the outward appearance of our lives; He can see every single thought that slips through our minds, and every attitude, desire, motive, and idea that we entertain in our hearts. Doesn't that bring a whole new light to things—God is watching our thought life and everything that goes on inside of us! He's watching us always. When we truly begin to *believe* that, we straighten up our act. We're being monitored under a whole new level of accountability!

In Matthew 23:28 Jesus tells the Pharisees, "So you, too, outwardly appear righteous to men, but inwardly you are full of hypocrisy and lawlessness." What about our motives? Are we serious about our walk with Christ because we want to please the Lord and strengthen our relationship with Him, or do we have ulterior motives? Is personal gain, such as building a "Christian image," included in our goal? Fame, money, and image are big snares that can skew our motives; we'd be wise to carefully avoid these traps.

As we take a step back and evaluate our lives, total purity begins to look impossible. Even if we're pure on the outside, we still have impurity on the inside. It's nearly impossible to tell if the motives behind our actions are completely pure. We try and try and try to live a pure life, but we mess up and fail—every single day. Maybe we've even made some big mistakes in regard to purity. *Is there any hope?*

With Jesus, there is always hope. You see, it's not *us* that makes us pure. It's Jesus in us. First John 1:7 says, "If we walk in the Light as He Himself is in the Light, we have fellowship with one another, and the blood of Jesus His Son cleanses us from all sin." There is *power in the blood,* friends. When we become Christians and Jesus enters our hearts, we are made new! We are made whole! We are made pure! From that point on, Jesus begins His sanctifying work in our lives.

Many times, our lives are full of sin and we don't even realize it. Even though we Christians have been given a new nature, our flesh still wants to live in its "glory days," wallowing in sin and even downright lewdness. Jeremiah 17:9 tells us the hard truth about the heart: "The heart is more deceitful than all else and is desperately sick; who can understand it?" We can't understand it, that's for sure. How did all that impurity get there? Sure, bad outside influences can fuel the fire, but Jesus says in Mark 7:18–23 that the evil comes from within our hearts. We were born sinful—that's why we need Jesus to save us!

But even as Christians, we stumble. Purity is still a struggle. We still sometimes sin. Ephesians 4:22–23 (NKJV) instructs us to "put off, concerning your former conduct, the old man which grows corrupt according to the deceitful lusts, and be renewed in the spirit of your mind." Note the phrase "put off"—we need to put off our sin nature; it won't just naturally fall off! We have to make our lives free from contamination. But how, in a world so determined to lure us into all the sin it has to offer, can we possibly do this? "How can a young person stay on the path of purity? By living according to your word" (Psalm 119:9 NIV).

Even when we mess up, Jesus is there to wash us clean. The story of Jesus washing His disciples' feet (found in John 13:5–11) is symbolic of how Jesus washes us when we get spiritually "dirty." In John 13:10 Jesus tells us that we are made clean because of Him (that's when we become saved), but we still need Him to wash our feet. As we walk through life, our feet can get dirty, and we need Jesus' constant forgiveness and cleansing blood in and over our lives.

Going back to Jeremiah 17, what of that deceitful heart that keeps trying to live in sin, even after we've been delivered from it? Verse 10 reads, "I, the LORD, search the heart, I test the mind." That, my friends, is a comforting thought. We may not be able to decipher our own hearts, minds, motives, and emotions, but the Lord sees everything crystal clear. He spots the impurity—and He can help us clean it up.

I know firsthand there's no way we girls can make sense of the emotional roller coaster we're on during our teen years, complete with raging hormones, scatterbrained thoughts, and romanticized notions. I can't tell you how often I have prayed straight out of Psalm 139:23–24 (NKJV), "Search me, O God, and know my heart; try me, and know my anxieties; and see if there is any wicked way in me, and lead me in the way everlasting."

True purity *does not* mean we have never committed a single sin. It's too late for that. But it does mean that we are clean because of the perfect, spotless Lamb living in our hearts—that's Jesus, and He's washing us clean every day. He's sanctifying us and making us pure as we walk through life with Him. We may get dirty here and there, but Jesus will forgive us if we repent before Him. In fact, He's even interceding for us (Romans 8:34)! He is *for* us! Living according to the Word of God, walking in the Spirit and not in the flesh, and being led every step of the way by the Holy Spirit—now that's what anyone would call an exceptional way of life.

PERSONAL (OR GROUP) QUESTIONS

1. What areas of impurity (in your own life or in general) have you dismissed as socially acceptable or "okay" because they are not generally seen as "bad"? How does God's Word affirm the black-and-whiteness of sin and righteousness regarding those areas?

2. How can you be pure in body, mind, soul, and spirit—not just in public, but before the Lord, living with integrity?

3. Why do you think it is hard to accept the Lord's forgiveness in the area of purity? Is there any sin you need to repent of and release to the Lord?

Today's Challenge

We've all messed up in regard to purity somehow, inside or out. Sometimes it can be hard to accept the forgiveness God graciously lavishes on us when we repent. Read King David's plea for purity and forgiveness in Psalm 51. Purpose to be pure—scour the scriptures for truths that reveal God's strong heart for purity. Then find scriptures on forgiveness. We need to know both.

Create in me a pure heart O GOD... Psalm 51:10

Delighting Yourself in the Lord

Delight yourself in the Lord; and He will give you the desires of your heart.
PSALM 37:4

Psalm 37:4 is the type of verse you'd find on a mug or the cover of a journal. I even have a shirt that says it in pretty script letters. It's a good verse, of course, but I think many of us read it the wrong way. We list the desires of our heart, whether new friends, a guy, a car, beauty, money, fame—and we assume God owes us our wish list because we delight in Him. But God's gifts don't depend on whether we're on the "Nice List." God delights in giving gifts (the best one being salvation!) without merit—just because He loves us. So what of Psalm 37:4? Let's break it down.

"Delight yourself in the Lord": to delight in someone means to take great pleasure in them. That's a radical concept right there—taking absolute pleasure in Jesus to where He is number one in our hearts, minds, and agendas. He is all we want, all we need, the only One we care to please. His love, His thoughts, His words, His gifts, His commands, His praises, His disciplines, and His presence are our favorites and we hold them in the highest importance. Nothing can steal our joy, identity, purpose, confidence, love for Him and for others—we are secure in the Creator of the universe, whom we also call Father, friend, and Lord. And He calls us "into His marvelous light" (1 Peter 2:9). He completes us (Colossians 2:10).

Can you wrap your mind around what it would look like to live your life *delighting yourself in the Lord?* Frankly, the world needs more Christians like this—Christians who have utter joy in the Lord that fuels a passion to live life for the kingdom of heaven (Nehemiah 8:10). Life doesn't get any better than living an adventure with your best friend. I don't know about you, but I want my relationship with God to be one of mutual delight. I want to delight in the Lord wholeheartedly. After all, He has already been delighting in me for quite a while now (Isaiah 62:4).

If we delight in the Lord, we worship Him—and that's exactly what we were created to do: bring God glory by worshipping Him with our whole lives. If we delight in the Lord, we obey His commands and fear Him. We take Him seriously and follow Him wherever He goes. Think about the Song of Solomon: that book of the Bible isn't just about a husband-and-wife relationship. It symbolizes our relationship with God—how He delights in us and how we should delight in Him! He calls us away from distractions to delight in Him alone and enjoy His peaceful presence. He longs to have our whole heart—our whole life!

Song of Solomon 8:6–7 talks about a strong, jealous love that cannot be quenched—that describes the tremendous love with which God pursues us. It's strong. It's jealous. And it's completely unquenchable; it's like a hungry fire devouring a forest, simply refusing to be put out. A love like this can't be shared. If we want to delight ourselves in the Lord, we can't be delighting ourselves in other things—like the world, like sin. James 4:4 tells it like it is: if we try to be friends with the world *and* with God, it's basically adultery. We can be friends with either the world or with God, but we have to take our pick. We must be friends with one and enemies with the other.

Back to Psalm 37:4: What about that part, "and He will give you the desires of your heart"? I don't think this verse limits God to simply blessing us with earthly gifts and fulfilling our tangible wants. Every person, deep within his or her being, is hardwired with the desire to be loved and accepted, no strings attached. To have purpose, belonging, and identity. And what of us girls? We want someone to tell us how beautiful we are. How much we matter to that person. How fervently we are loved. We want to find unwavering security in someone.

Many people plunge their lives off the deep end searching to fulfill these desires—and after every temporary fix they try, they resurface empty, confused, and hurting more than ever. That's because nothing in this world can satisfy us, and delight us like Jesus can. We find true peace and satisfaction when He is Lord of our lives and we delight in Him. We were made to be fulfilled by Jesus—that's why He is enough.

When we truly delight in the Lord—glorying in who He is and rejoicing like the bride in the Song of Solomon (6:3), declaring, "I am my beloved's and my beloved is mine," and actively, passionately taking part in the abiding relationship we were meant to have with Him, *He Himself meets the desires of our heart.* In Him we find those desires met. In Him we find love, joy, peace, meaning, purpose, and fulfillment. You know what's going to make us truly satisfied? Not popularity or fame. Not money or success. Not even marriage or a fairy tale. The ultimate satisfaction comes from Jesus Himself *alone*.

So having the desires of our heart satisfied *results* from delighting in the Lord. It's completely true. But let's not trick ourselves into thinking that God doesn't gratify our wants at times. *God loves to give gifts!* He loves to grant our desires! But sometimes God won't give us what we want because He has something far better. He can see the future, and we can't. He knows what will happen, and we don't. He knows us better than we know ourselves. His timing, His way, and His plans are the absolute best! He has our best interests in mind!

It all boils down to trust. Delighting ourselves in the Lord can be a big, daunting, difficult leap of faith, especially for us girls as we're testing our wings and seeing how we fly in life. Do we trust God with the desires of our hearts? If we delight in Him, He will meet our needs. But do we even trust Him to meet *all* those needs and desires? What about the desire for a godly future husband? Uplifting, close-knit friendships? Adventurous opportunities? Health for a loved one or even ourselves? God gives and God takes away (Job 1:21). God can bless with and God can bless without. God may withhold from you *your* best—because He wants to give you *His* best.

We can't live life with deficits and holes, or we'll sink trying to fill them. A sincere delight in the One who loved us even while we were still sinners (Romans 5:8), who pursues us, even though we are unfaithful at times, and who sees beauty and worth in His precious, handmade creations—that is what will keep us afloat in life. Jesus in us makes us whole (Colossians 2:10).

1.   What things often attract your delight more than the Lord? Why do you think that is?

2.   Pinpoint some of the deepest specific needs and desires of your heart. Now think about how delighting 100 percent in Jesus satisfies them.

3.   What are some of the lies that get in your way of trusting God completely with your desires, hopes, and dreams? What are some scriptural promises that combat these lies with the truth?

Today's Challenge

Trust is one of the biggest keys to delighting in the Lord. Find and write out Bible verses specific to those areas of your life that you struggle to trust God with. Put them in places where you'll see them often, and anytime you're discouraged, speak those verses out loud and believe them firmly.

PSALM 37:four

Delight
YOURSELF in the
Lord & HE
WILL give YOU the
desires of your heart.

The Truth about Your Heart

"For where your treasure is, there your heart will be also."
LUKE 12:34

Life, it seems, hardly gets more romantic than the dangerous Canadian frontier of the early nineteenth century—my mom, my sister Genevieve, and I were immediately drawn into the Hallmark TV series *When Calls the Heart.* (We do enjoy a good chick flick!) I mean, who *doesn't* love it when a rich city girl turned small-town schoolteacher falls for a shy but charming and brave Mountie? In fact, basically everyone who enters the tiny Canadian town of Hope Valley finds true love. Why, you ask? Because it's the central theme of the series: *Your heart called you here—so follow it.*

Whoa, red flag—*follow your heart?* My heart? The one God's Word describes as "deceitful" and "desperately wicked" (Jeremiah 17:9 NKJV)? I don't think so. As much as I enjoy a good show like *When Calls the Heart* for entertainment, shows like this don't provide much in the way of realistic advice. Ladies, listen up: *Never follow your heart.* It's not worth the risk. I know, it sounds terribly unromantic and pessimistic, but don't take my word for it. Let's examine the cold, hard facts straight from the ultimate source of truth, right here in Jeremiah 17:9 (NKJV): "The heart is deceitful above all things, and desperately wicked; who can know it?" Here's what I'm picking up on:

- *Deceitful.* As girls, we can probably all concur with the deceitfulness of our hearts. Sometimes it feels like our heart is playing tricks on us—our feelings change by the minute. Things can become one big mess of internal noise: *I was just positive he and I were meant to be. I thought I really liked him. I thought he* really liked me. I was sure God told me to do XYZ—that this was His plan—that this was the right thing. She used to be easier to get along with. Mom and Dad were so much more reasonable back then. I didn't know I was capable of sin like that. Does God love me? Is what I know true? Have I changed? What's wrong with me? Am I normal? Who am I? It seems our hearts are inventing new whims to chase every few minutes—along with plenty of extreme emotions to go with them. Can't they ever stop being fickle long enough for us to actually decipher what on earth is going on inside of them?

- *Desperately wicked.* We were born with the curse of evil seething through our fallen human DNA—Psalm 51:5 has it right—and now we're telling ourselves to live at the mercy of that heart so innately bent on wickedness? Inclined toward opposing and defying its Creator? That heart from which we need saving? Whether we like it or not, sin is wired into our hearts as a default. Paul describes this inner struggle with himself in Romans 7:21, 24: "I find then the principle that evil is present in me, the one who wants to do good. . . . Wretched man that I am! Who will set me free from the body of this death?"

And then we're left with that final question: *"Who can know it?"* (Jeremiah 17:9 NKJV, emphasis mine). Well, thankfully, the suspense is short lived. The very next verse goes on to enlighten us: "I, the LORD, search the heart, I test the mind, even to give every man according to his ways, according to the fruit of his doings" (17:10 NKJV). Praise the Lord that He knows how to untangle the jumbled mess in my heart and make sense of it—because I sure don't. I've tried and I've failed. God is the only One who can know our hearts—and He can bring us clarity to see things the way He sees them: in an orderly (not a confusing) way.

Admittedly, our heart has some problems, but the great news is that when we became Christians, Jesus replaced our dark, filthy, crazy heart with a brand-new heart inhabited by His presence! If we've made the decision to turn from our sins and trust in the Lord, our heart has been transformed from a haunted house full of evil to a home where Jesus abides. He saves us from our sins by getting right to the heart of the matter, if you know what I mean (Mark 7:20–22).

Yes, our heart may still be kind of dirty at first, but His presence and love begin to clean up the mess and make repairs. Just like Paul talked about in Romans 7, however, we have a battle of wills waging within us. Our old heart (the flesh) doesn't want to give up and get out so easily. Our flesh tries to peep through every now and then and take over our heart.

Even so, the Holy Spirit within us is stronger, and if we let Him, He can win over the flesh any day. But often it takes some stubborn, stand-your-ground fight. A prayer like Psalm 139:23–24 is a lifesaver in times of spiritual cardiac arrest. Can't figure out the spiritual tangles in your heart? Neither can I. So let's take them to the One who can deal with them—let's allow Him to search us, convict us, and refine us through His loving truth and correction.

Our heart is Jesus' home, which makes it a vital part of our lives. Proverbs 4:23 (NIV) stresses the importance of guarding our hearts with care and vigilance: "Above all else, guard your heart, for everything you do flows from it." We must guard those precious hearts of ours by making sure nothing gets through the gate that isn't fit for our King. Tighten the security, check the alarms, watch those gates to your heart—your eyes, ears, and mind—and be sure to filter everything you see, hear, and think through the Word of God. Does it meet the standards of Philippians 4:8? Is that movie, that song, that conversation, that image going to help your heart become a cleaner, purer, better home for Jesus, or is it garbage that will get between you and the Lord?

We need to guard the thoughts we allow ourselves to entertain. It's one thing to wonder when God's best choice of a Mr. Right is going to sweep us off our feet. It's another to idolize the idea of romance in our every waking thought. It's natural to wonder if we are beautiful, and even quite all right to be happy with the way God made our physical appearance. But we've gone too far when we become vainly consumed and altogether distracted by our looks, whether we completely love or detest them. See what I mean? When a thought becomes unhealthy and morally corrupting and pulls us away from Christ, we'd be wise to pull out the big guns—scripture and prayer—and fight against anything getting in the way of purity, humility, truth, and the love of Christ.

"You shall love the Lord your God with all your heart. . . ." The greatest commandment (Matthew 22:37) is, in fact, our heart's greatest help. When we love the Lord and His commandments (Psalm 119:47) and value them above all else, then our hearts find joy and health. We will love others, be grateful and content, and know true peace when we love the Lord and have full confidence in the trustworthiness of Him and His Word.

Luke 12:34 is the key to this truth: "For where your treasure is, there your heart will be also." Our heart will follow what we value. Rather than following our heart to find the truth, we must lead our heart to follow the things we know to be true. Our heart won't lead us to our happiest, meant-to-be destiny, but we can lead our hearts to follow a path that aligns with God's flawless plan. His plan is beautiful, perfect, and nothing short of amazing.

So knowing the truth about our hearts isn't at all about crushing dreams and taking the sparkle out of our future. The silver screen can keep inventing debonair princes and romanticizing the frontier, but these stories don't begin to compare with the real, significant, deep, beautiful love stories God can write. We girls can allow our emotions to get the best of us, or we can stand firm on God's Word and trek forward to follow Him. You and me, we can do this, because Someone is living on the throne of our hearts who enables us to live life to the fullest. Next time we're tempted to follow our hearts into the shaky wonderland of indecipherable feelings and emotions, we'll stand our ground and say, "Heart, follow Him!"

PERSONAL (OR GROUP) QUESTIONS

1. What are some of the lies about following your heart that you've heard through the media or the culture? In contrast, what is the truth of God's Word?

2. When are you most tempted to follow your heart?

3. Have you ever experienced a time when you followed your heart, it misled you, and you wished you had sought the Lord instead?

Today's Challenge

We girls love a good love story, right? Ironically enough, most of the love stories we watch are not, well, good. They're fake, overglamorized, often cheesy, and nothing like real, God-centered love. Desire to experience someday the kind of love story written by the Author of love Himself—God! Search your Bible for verses on true love and pure, godly relationships, and pray that the Lord would give you His heart for love, romance, and purity. His way is always best.

FOR WHERE YOUR *treasure* IS, THERE YOUR *will be also*

LUKE 12:34

Guys

Treat younger men as brothers. . .and younger women as sisters, with absolute purity.
1 Timothy 5:1–2 niv

If you're looking for the answers to all your boy problems, there are way better books sold at your local Christian bookstore that are entirely devoted to the subject. What in the world do I have to say about a topic like boys? I have five sisters and zero brothers—even our pets are females. I hardly had a normal conversation with a boy until I was about fourteen. I don't have a whole lot of field experience with them. Basically, I'm still trying to figure things out. But really, which girl isn't? We wouldn't have guy questions or problems if we had already mastered the fine art of classy and proper interaction with young men.

Take it from a die-hard romantic: I find the innate chemistry between guys and girls fascinating. God's designs are just so good and perfect. From a young age, we feel that instinctive gravitational pull to the profusely intriguing opposite gender. We're completely different, yes, yet beautifully complementary; deep inside of us, we know we are meant to be together. To love each other forever. To attract and be attracted. We long for intimate companionship. We desire to be at some special guy's side, to be back next to that rib cage we were taken from (Genesis 2:22), taking on the world together.

Do you ever wonder if God is too busy to care about things as trivial as our love life? I mean, He's the King of the universe! There are wars, poverty, eight billion souls and counting on this planet alone—does He truly care about our interactions with guys? The answer is *yes*—significantly! The God who takes care of nations also takes care of sparrows and flowers (Matthew 6:25–34). He desires to be a part of every relationship and interaction we have. Billy Graham put it like this: "God is more interested in your future and your relationships than you are."

I definitely don't have all the answers to everything, but I do know where they're all kept: the Bible. God's Word, though old, is far from outdated. As the ultimate source of truth, it can help us navigate even the trickiest things life throws at us when we have the Holy Spirit as our guide.

I know I'm not the only girl who dreams of her wedding day. Well, really, I'm wondering about this groom fella—who is he? More than likely, you and I both have future husbands who are real, live guys doing life somewhere on earth right now, and eventually, in God's perfect timing, our paths will cross. What a crazy thought! It's all so exciting I can hardly stand the suspense. It's as bad as Christmas morning when we were seven—whatever are we supposed to do while we wait? Proverbs 31—a chapter all about being a godly woman—says that a godly wife "does [her husband] good and not evil all the days of her life" (Proverbs 31:12). Every single day of her life—even before she's met him. He's somewhere, right? How can we do our future Mr. Right *good* and not evil right now, as singles, preparing for a dynamic covenant marriage someday?

Guard your interactions with guys. Don't misunderstand me—it's quite all right and even healthy to have good, solid guy friendships! As Christians, guys and girls are brothers and sisters in Christ. We share the same Father. And like any good sister, we can do our part to help our brothers walk in victory in a world that is becoming increasingly hostile to purity. It's far too easy for any of us to stumble and fall.

Our friendships with guys will look a bit different than with girls. With girls, we might spend excessive amounts of time doing excessive amounts of talking as we eat excessive amounts of chocolate. We value close heart-to-heart friendships with our sisters in Christ. To have mutually uplifting guy friendships, however, our interactions with guys need to be distinctly more casual and distant than with our girlfriends. Someday I want to marry my absolute best friend—so I am saving that title for my future husband.

"Above all else, guard your heart, for everything you do flows from it" (Proverbs 4:23 NIV)—a classic verse that we normally pull up when talking about guys, girls, and matters of the heart. How can we guard our own hearts, help protect the hearts of our brothers in Christ, and do our future husband good? While there are zillions of things we could cover, here are a few yeas and nays concerning how to be a helpful, godly sister:

- *HELPFUL: Conduct yourself with honor and purity.* Proverbs 20:11 says our conduct speaks for who we are. The Lord calls us to purity, not to the filth and immorality He paid such a high price to free us from. First Timothy 5:1–2 directs us to treat one another like family, in purity.
- *HELPFUL: Show some respect for yourself.* Be kind and respectable. Dress honorably—modesty should be an outward reflection of the beautiful work God is doing inside of us, rather than simply a set of rules to follow. We should honor the Lord and point to Him rather than drawing inappropriate attention to our body. Modesty shows respect first for the Lord, then for ourselves, and finally for those around us.
- *HELPFUL: Commend chivalry.* Thank him for opening the door for you, for walking you through the parking lot, for helping you carry that immensely heavy object you had in your arms. Smile at the relieving fact that chivalry is still alive, though it may be rare. Encourage the men around you to be real, godly men and leaders in a culture that calls their God-given role repulsive.
- *HELPFUL: Be just a little picky.* In context, of course: don't give every self-proclaimed Prince Charming your number. Have standards for whom you will allow to pursue you, and be sure to screen each potential suitor through your dad (or another trusted Christian spiritual leader) first! That will help weed out the creepers and determine character.
- *NOT HELPFUL: Demeaning feministic comments.* Enough with the "we-can-do-anything-men-can-do-better-and-in-high-heels" business. I know that's not true—I have blistered feet as I write. Comments about females being superior and men being annoying or dumb do not in any way encourage our brothers toward godliness, manliness, and leadership.

They simply encourage passivity, and they're just plain mean.

- *NOT HELPFUL: Flirtatiousness and "leading him on."* When we respond to every single text and spend every waking moment with a guy, we are sending the message "I like you." Even if we're just friends. And then the trouble begins. Things get confusing. He gets hurt. We feel bad.
- *NOT HELPFUL: Missionary dating.* Just don't date anyone who's not a Christian. Period. See 2 Corinthians 6:14. It never works out, outside of the Hallmark Channel.

Speaking of dates, be sure to respect your parents' rules and boundaries, no matter how archaic your friends say they are. Families will have different opinions about how relationships ought to play out, but ultimately, we must seek to honor the Lord first, in our hearts and with our actions. Pray for your future husband and do him good right where you are. Save your very best for him—don't waste your time on guys who won't be there for you in the long run.

God has probably already blessed you with guys in your life right now, like a dad or brothers. Develop your relationships with the men in your family so you can openly talk about guys with them, getting their insight and feedback. And of course, talk to the Lord about your heart. About your guy friends. About your desires. About the man you will marry someday. As romantic as we hope our future love story will be, no man can complete us, no matter how perfect the fit. We are already completed—Jesus Christ makes us whole (Colossians 2:10).

PERSONAL (OR GROUP) QUESTIONS

1. What do you find the hardest about relating to guys in a God-honoring, siblings-in-Christ kind of way? Are there any brother or father figures in your life who can encourage you and give you advice in this area of life?

2. In what ways have you been a helpful (or unhelpful) sister in Christ? What are ways you can encourage your brothers in Christ to be godly men?

3. How can you pray for your future husband this week?

Today's Challenge

I've heard it recommended to write letters to your future husband, which I enjoyed doing...for about the first two letters, and then I didn't really know what to say to this nameless, faceless, unknown fella. But what I have found very helpful is writing out prayers to the Lord for my future husband. It reminds me to pray for him and catalogs what I've prayed about. Designate a journal for prayers and start talking to the Lord about the man whom He has for you someday.

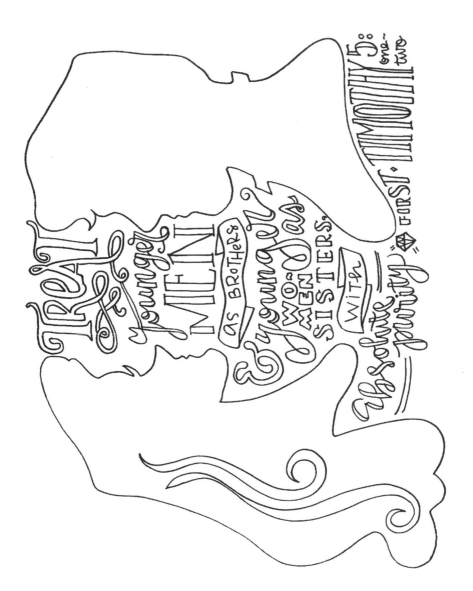

TREAT younger MEN as brothers, younger women as sisters, with absolute purity ~ FOR 1ST · TIMOTHY 5: one~two

Beware of Idols

Little children, guard yourselves from idols.
1 JOHN 5:21

Did you know that the God we serve as Christians—the one and only true God—is a jealous God? He wants our hearts completely to Himself, and He doesn't want to share them with anybody else.

The first two of the Ten Commandments clearly state:

1. "You shall have no other gods before Me" (Exodus 20:3).
2. "You shall not make for yourself an idol. . . . You shall not worship them or serve them; for I, the LORD your God, am a jealous God" (Exodus 20:4–5).

Well, obviously! Idol worship is primitive business—or so we think. We often think of idols as being Buddha statues, golden calves, or strange entities like hawks with human features (or something like that) worshipped by cannibals in the heart of somewhere completely secluded from civilization. And maybe, just maybe, if we're being insightful, we include Canadian pop stars in this category.

The truth is, idolatry doesn't hit as far from home as we may think. We may not bow down to Baal or pledge our allegiance to Zeus, but who—or what—has our heart? Who has our worship, our undivided allegiance and focus? Who defines us and determines how we live our lives? Who is number one in our lives?

The natural answer for us Christians to program ourselves with is "Jesus." But if we're honest with ourselves, He's often not number one on the list. And friends, if we can't answer "Jesus" to the questions above with full confidence and utter honesty, we have an idol worship situation in our lives that needs to be promptly taken care of.

I'll be the first to admit that it's way too easy to let idols creep into our hearts and slowly remove Jesus from the number one spot in our lives. Look at the last words in John's first epistle: "Little children, guard yourselves from idols" (1 John 5:21). Obviously, if we weren't in danger of falling into idolatry, we wouldn't need to guard ourselves.

The idols in our lives don't usually look as blatant or pagan as golden statues. They often look like social lives, the world, culture, jobs, celebrities, hobbies, significant others, friends, family, dreams for the future, habits, and—more than likely—ourselves. It's the grave truth. It's usually not a false god from another religion that we begin to worship—it's usually us. We're the idols in our own hearts. When we put ourselves, our agendas, and our way above God and His Word, we make idols of ourselves.

So what do we do? By now it's pretty clear after looking at God's Word that He hates idolatry (in Deuteronomy 27:15, He calls it an *abomination*, and when God uses that word, it means He *firmly, passionately hates it*), and it's also pretty clear that most of us have idols in our lives. Guilty as charged.

Praise be to God, He is faithful and merciful to us always. Even when we have allowed idols into our lives, He still loves us and walks through the dethroning of these idols with us. He wants our hearts to turn back to Him and longs for us to give Him the number one spot again, because His heart breaks when we leave our first love (Revelation 2:4). Here are three ideas for how to make Jesus your number one priority:

1. *Give Him the first and best of your time.* We willingly devote a lot of time to someone or something that is important and valuable to us. Die-hard athletes spend hours upon hours devoted to their sport. Musicians peg (or pluck) away at their practice time to get better and better. Time spent with a close friend is enjoyable and refreshing and draws you even closer together.

It's no different with God. How much time do we spend with God? Does He get the best part of our day, the top slot in our schedule? Or does He get whatever we have left after social, school, church, work, and family activities? It's something to consider: How can God possibly be number one in our lives if we don't put any time into growing closer to Him? Whether that looks like waking up thirty minutes earlier or scheduling a set time into our routine, we have some daily catching up to do with God.

2. *Talk to God about it.* Instead of trying to tackle idols in our lives all alone, let's take them to the Lord who put that innate desire to worship within our hearts. Talk to Him about the things you idolize. Repent, asking for forgiveness and for Him to help you love Him with all your heart, soul, mind, and strength. Remember, we can't change ourselves. When it comes to changing our hearts, God does all the heavy lifting. Talk to Him in general. Obviously, we talk to people we value and love. Prayer strengthens our relationship with God and is an act of relying on Him rather than ourselves.

3. *Knock down your idols and pursue the Lord with everything you have.* It's time to get real with ourselves about what we've turned into an idol and who God really is. Fight those false gods with the truth: It is a blessing to have an education and a job, but those don't come before the Lord. In fact, they pale in comparison to knowing the Creator of the universe (Psalms 25:14; 100:3). Those friends are sweet, fun, encouraging people to be around, but they are still human and will sometimes let us down and not be there for us. Our God is always faithful, even when we're not, and He will never fail us or leave us (Hebrews 13:5). See how it's done?

Finally, seek the Lord with all your heart. James 4:8 promises, "Draw near to God and He will draw near to you." What are some practical ways we can draw near to God? We read God's Word, the Bible, daily, hungrily, meticulously, and joyfully. We pray fervent prayers with full confidence that He's listening. We praise Him with our actions, our words, our hearts, our thoughts, and our songs. And we experience the joy of being truly fulfilled—after all, who needs idols when you know the one true God personally?

PERSONAL (OR GROUP) QUESTIONS

1. What things have you made into idols? What consumes most of your time? How can you cast down those idols?

2. What sorts of things does culture say should come first (be our idols) because they will satisfy us? How does Jesus outshine them and truly satisfy us?

3. What are some practical ways you can put Jesus first in your life?

Today's Challenge

Search your heart—and maybe your schedule—to determine what is consuming your every thought, desire, spare moment. Are there any idols you need to get rid of? Things like social media, money, beauty, even hanging out with friends—none of which are inherently evil things—can become idols if we allow them to become more important than our time and our relationship with the Lord. Ask God to help you put Him completely first in your life.

Little children, GUARD YOURSELVES from

1 John 5:21

Selfishness

In everything give thanks; for this is God's will for you in Christ Jesus.
1 Thessalonians 5:18

It starts with a nagging itch inside, an itch for fairness. . .but we'll settle for superiority. An itch to be like—or to have more than—someone else. I mean, if they get it, so should I, *right*? Am I the only one who's ever experienced the burn of jealousy? I didn't think so. We are pros at the game of envy, comparison, and entitlement. We show symptoms of this innate disease called "the flesh"—and they run deep. Galatians 5:19–21 says, "Now the deeds of the flesh are evident, which are. . .jealousy. . .envying. . .and things like these, of which I forewarn you, just as I have forewarned you, that those who practice such things will not inherit the kingdom of God." Life isn't fair—we hear it again and again, but we just can't accept that. *Why does* she, *and not* me*?*

Few feelings are more terribly annoying than *jealousy*. It is selfish, and it doesn't like to see somebody else being so blessed: She won the scholarship. Got a boyfriend. Landed the lead role. Became friends with our best friend. Makes more money at her fun job. Gets a lot of attention. Is very successful. And. . .we don't like it, because we don't have it and we don't want her to have it. Her success almost makes us angry—why her? We don't like that someone else is winning at life (as if it were a competition).

James 3:16 tells us a startling truth: "For where jealousy and selfish ambition exist, there is disorder and every evil thing." When individuals are so bent on their own selfishness—no matter the cost to others—they quit playing by the rules. They forget—or disregard—God's words in Philippians 2:3: "Do nothing from selfishness or empty conceit, but with humility of mind regard one another as more important than yourselves." Just as humility fosters good relationships, jealousy kills them. It eats away at us and, if we nurture it, turns us bitter.

A close companion to jealousy is *comparison*. An absolute killjoy, party pooper, and gratefulness zapper. I mean, who can possibly be content with what they have when they're competitively comparing themselves to the girls around them: Who has the best body? Who's prettier? Who has a cooler family? Who has a better boyfriend? You know the old saying: whoever dies with the most toys *still dies*. Comparison takes our eyes off all that God has done for us, all He's freely given us, and all He's blessed us with. Instead, it focuses on the temporal—what everyone else has—even if it's not much better! But we feel entitled to it instead of them. Nothing will quench our happiness quicker than a glance around the room with our eyes wide open to the things we haven't been blessed with. And boy, it's frustrating that someone else has.

Girls throughout history have been guilty of comparison, but I think our generation takes the cake. I'm sure there was a time when people compared hoop-skirts, bonnets, and carriages at church picnics, but now, nearly every day, we hop on our various social media sites and scroll through countless posts about all the awesome things our friends and acquaintances are doing. Scrolling through the highlights of others can make our own lives feel pathetic and dull. We can be deceived into thinking that everyone else is always on vacation, looking their A-plus best, doing fun things. . .while we're sitting at home waiting for our life to start being that exhilarating. But social media is only a collection of the best Kodak moments snapped. A picture may say a thousand words, but it doesn't tell the full story about a person's life. Generally, someone's reality is far less back-to-back thrilling than it appears on our smartphone. A number of likes or comments isn't an accurate gauge of how happy or fulfilled this person feels. Be careful with comparison, especially on social media. Not everything is as it seems!

Entitlement—a good vocabulary word, perfect for my generation. It's a sure-fire method to avoid any traces of thankfulness if we ingrain it into our mindset. It's why I sobbed my eyes out because I was the only kid in fourth grade who didn't have a cell phone. Or Facebook account. Or the most Webkinz animals (best toy ever in my elementary years). See, entitlement looks at wants and calls them needs. It takes for granted blessings, because it says, "I deserve this."

As young women, we might feel entitled to popularity, respect, relationships, possessions, money from our parents, invitations, expensive gifts, trips, the list goes on and on. Often we ask God egocentric questions such as, "Why did You make me look like this?" As if we are entitled to have a say in looking some other way. "Why haven't you shown me Your plan?" As if we are entitled to answers. "Why did You bring her a guy, and I'm still single?" As if we are entitled to relationships, marriage, or the things someone else has.

Jealousy, comparison, and entitlement—three different traits with one shared focus: looking out for numero uno. But I think our motivation goes even deeper: Do we think God has forgotten us? Do we doubt His goodness toward us and feel defensive when we see His goodness toward others? Friends, God will *never* stop loving us and being good toward us. Your life is different than mine; my life is different than yours. God has us both specifically in mind as He thoughtfully grants and withholds certain privileges in our lives—perhaps for a time or for good—for our absolute best interest, in His perfect plan. He delights in blessing us with His best. First Peter 5:6 gives us some wise advice: "Therefore humble yourselves under the mighty hand of God, that He may exalt you at the proper time." Rather than letting your flesh take the wheel, humbly surrender all control to the Lord, knowing that He is sovereign and does indeed have the whole world in His hands. Let Him be the one to bring blessings and exaltation in His perfect timing.

God is good. Meditate on those three words rather than entertaining rivalry in your heart toward your sisters in Christ. Like Romans 12:15 says, "Rejoice with those who rejoice." Learn to celebrate the blessings in the lives of others. Let joy overtake you when you hear of the good God is doing for someone. Choose to thank the Lord for His kind generosity in their lives and in your own, rather than belittling the great things He's done for someone else. Inspire others to thankfulness and celebration rather than knocking the blessings you're jealous of.

And of course, remember how you have been blessed yourself. Ditch the entitlement. Did you get any birthday presents this year? Be thankful—what a blessing to have people who think of us on our special day. Did you have any meals today? Did you do any massive loads of laundry? Be thankful—what a blessing it is to have our basic needs met. But you know what makes us thankful? It's not necessarily the fact that we have something that someone else doesn't. It's when we acknowledge the fact that you and I do have something. If you died today, would you go to heaven? Be thankful—Jesus made that possible, and we have received His truth. He loves us hugely—and knowing that, how can we help but be content?

PERSONAL (OR GROUP) QUESTIONS

1. What are some blessings in your life that blow your mind with gratefulness? What about ones you take for granted?
2. When do you find it easiest to get pulled into the comparison game?
3. Think of someone who is going through a joyful time in life right now—maybe someone you have been tempted to be jealous of. What are ways you can fight jealous feelings and thank God for His goodness in that person's life?

Today's Challenge

Start a list of blessings in your life that you are thankful to God for. Keep it in a place where you can add to it and look back on it when you are tempted to be jealous or compare.

In everything give THANKS; for this is God's will for you in Christ Jesus.

I Thessalonians 5:18

Humility

The reward of humility and the fear of the Lᴏʀᴅ are riches, honor and life.
Pʀᴏᴠᴇʀʙs 22:4

Humility—the secret serum to happy relationships, a key that unlocks greater happiness, and a magnet that draws others to the difference they see in us. No, we don't have to eat humble pie to have a humble heart. In fact, God-honoring humility takes pride in the truth that we have nothing meaningful to offer the world without Jesus. And because of that, humility is secure and confident in the Lord's might and marvelousness, completely satisfied with who God made us to be. And on top of that, humility seeks to put others first because we acknowledge the true value and intricate depth that God has endowed them with.

Romans 12:3 (ɴɪᴠ) directs the Christ follower, "Do not think of yourself more highly than you ought, but rather think of yourself with sober judgment." It's high time to sober up from being drunk on ourselves—we're not seeing the facts straight. In fact, a girl doesn't need to have high self-esteem to be full of her own selfish interest. Pride manifests itself in many forms. It's human nature to feel entitled to bigger and better things and to look out for number one first—everyone else can be number two. Whether we think we're all that or, at the other extreme, we view ourselves as an object of hate, a mind hyperconsumed with serving ourselves is a sure sign of pride.

Pride often gets the best of most people, including me. Sometimes it's all too easy to put myself before others, even in my heart and mind. When it comes to humility, few chapters are more convicting than Philippians 2—the chapter that talks about Jesus Christ's humility. As God in the flesh, He had every right to demand the treatment rightly owed to God. But He chose the opposite—to be a servant to others, plain and ordinary, and to humble Himself before His Father, ready to submit and do whatever would bring more glory to the Father, even if that meant death. And what did God do? He lifted Jesus' name high. He exalted Him. If Jesus, the perfect Son of God, humbled Himself, how much more should we, as merely imperfect humans, follow His example of humility?

Pride can destroy relationships. It says, "I'm better than you. I deserve best. My needs and wants are most important of all." What if, instead, you and I sought to be examples of humility, like Jesus, and put ourselves *last*? What if we truly lived by Philippians 2:3–4: "Do nothing from selfishness or empty conceit, but with humility of mind regard one another as more important than yourselves; do not merely look out for your own personal interests, but also for the interests of others." Humility takes the lowly position. It doesn't have to win every argument. It can rejoice with others instead of fuming in jealousy. It cares about the needs of others.

I'd be leaving out some prime information without recognizing that pride is ultimately a sin against God. Whether we find it in our relationships, our decisions, or even our thoughts, pride boils down to an ugly state where we exalt ourselves above the One who should be exalted above all. We must decide who's boss, who sits on the throne of our hearts, and who calls the shots: us or God.

Proverbs 16:18 speaks straight truth: "Pride goes before destruction, and a haughty spirit before stumbling." Read the story of Adam and Eve. The cutest and happiest (and only) couple on earth desired godlike status enough to choose their way over God's explicit commands—enter sin and suffering to plague humanity. King Pharaoh dared to defy the almighty God and enslave His holy people—and he lost everything in the process. King Nebuchadnezzar took credit for what the Lord had done in his life, and the next thing you know, he was grazing in the fields in the humbling state of a wild animal (Daniel 4:28–37).

God hates pride (Proverbs 8:13). He cannot tolerate direct defiance of His commands, because He knows it will only hurt us—pride can only end in destruction! How do we avoid a downfall? We humans have become addicted to our own ways, and rehabilitation seems nearly impossible. Yet the Bible gives us clear tips on how to honor God with humility instead of wallowing in unapologetic pride:

- *Be broken before God.* James 4:9 and Ecclesiastes 3:4 vouch for the words of Psalm 51:17: "The sacrifices of God are a broken spirit; a broken and a contrite heart, O God, You will not despise." Let sin break your heart. Humbly confessing our sins and acknowledging our sinful inclinations is a step toward brokenness, healing, and restoration.
- *Work out your salvation with fear and trembling.* Philippians 2:12 (AMP, brackets in original) talks expansively about the cautious, humble position believers ought to take before God: "Work out your salvation [that is, cultivate it, bring it to full effect, actively pursue spiritual maturity] with awe-inspired fear and trembling [using serious caution and critical self-evaluation to avoid anything that might offend God or discredit the name of Christ]."
- *Never put yourself above sin.* The moment we say, "I would never do that," is the moment we become susceptible to that sin. We let down our guards and loosen accountability. You and I are capable of any and every gross sin in the records. It is only by the fear of the Lord, the Holy Spirit within us, and the grace of God that we can resist temptation and walk in the righteousness of Jesus who lives in our hearts. We desperately need a healthy distrust of our own fallen human nature at all times, because it is a constant reminder of the only One we can trust. Like the old hymn goes, "I need Thee every hour."
- *Know your weaknesses and exalt the Lord.* Paul, one of the greatest Christian men ever, admitted to weakness—a "thorn in the flesh" (2 Corinthians 12:7) given to him to keep him humble. We all have weaknesses, but instead of letting them define us, decide our actions, and bring us down, we can let them be spotlights for God's strength to steal the show as He makes up for our insufficiency. The Holy Spirit living in us is why we can live life abundantly, free of sin and pride! "Therefore I am well content with

weaknesses. . .for Christ's sake," Paul says. "For when I am weak, then I am strong" (2 Corinthians 12:10).

Just to be clear, it's okay to be satisfied with a job well done and even to like the person God made you to be! Pride happens when the Lord is no longer above all in our lives and we are consumed with our own will. Still, it's important to keep a good heart and not let the praise of others puff us up. Learn the fine art of deflecting praise to whom it is really due. And remember, no matter how hard we work, no matter how many friends, family members, and piano teachers are involved, the Lord always gets all the praise, because without Him, we can do nothing. As we read in James 4:10 (NIV), "Humble yourselves before the Lord, and he will lift you up."

PERSONAL (OR GROUP) QUESTIONS

1. When is it hardest to humble yourself?
2. How do you respond when people praise you? How can you stay humble when you win or accomplish something?
3. What are some ways you can humble yourself before the Lord every day?

Today's Challenge

Find opportunities at home, at school, at work, at church—wherever—to intentionally put others' needs before your own.

The REWARD of humility & the FEAR of the LORD are RICHES, honor and LIFE.

PROVERBS 22:4

Ten Ways to Be a Great Friend

A friend loves at all times.
PROVERBS 17:17

We girls are very relationship-centric creatures—whether we're shy or extroverted, soft spoken or loud, we relish those deep, meaningful friendships with people who care about us, bring us joy, and take interest in who we are. Relationships and friendships will look different across the board—Christians, unbelievers, family, ministry friends, mentorships, girlfriends, guy friends, boyfriends, husbands, you name it—but in each one of these relationships we should seek to point others to Christ and to glorify God. We're His kids, after all (1 John 3:1)!

Our friendships with other sisters in Christ have the potential to be dynamic and to truly help shape us into stronger women of God (Proverbs 27:17) as we share in common the goal of serving Jesus. But whether a person is someone to *be friends with* or not, we can *be a friend* to everyone in any sort of relationship. And many times, when we're a good friend, others respond in mutual kindness and a friendship is born. As representatives for Christ (2 Corinthians 5:20), we should make sure every human interaction we engage in is saturated in God's agape (unconditional) love.

So what does being a true, godly friend look like? I can't pretend I'm an expert friend, but God sure knows all about friendship, and His Word has plenty to say on how to treat others. Here are ten tips for being a great friend:

1. *Treat her the way you want to be treated.* Matthew 7:12—the Golden Rule—is one of the most popular scripture verses, and yet very few people actually live by it. How do we want to be treated? Do we want

to be welcomed? Then let's welcome the new girl; she seems lonely and shy. Do we want to be gossiped about? No, so we'll speak kind words in front of her and behind her back. It's not rocket science to treat every person with respect and dignity—but it sure isn't second nature, either.

2. *Spur her on to be who God made her to be.* Our friends are full of talents, passions, dreams, and potential—God has called them (as He has called us) to something huge. We can help propel them forward in the exciting things God is doing in their lives. It means so much to me when a friend asks how my book writing is going, how the school semester has been, or how one of my latest projects is coming along. Having godly friends who are praying for you and cheering you on provides a burst of fresh motivation!

3. *Rejoice when she's rejoicing. Weep when she's weeping.* This is a big one— Romans 12:15 is a free nugget of gold. There's nothing admirable about apathy. A true friend will be there through the rejoicing and the weeping. She doesn't disappear when there's a trial and then show up when there's a party; she's there for the long haul.

   - When a friend is celebrating something wonderful going on in her life, like an answer to prayer, an opportunity, a milestone, or a relationship, we should celebrate right along with her! Get giddy over what she's giddy about. I love sharing my own excitement with friends who will squeal in high-pitched tones right along with me.

   - Sadly, there will be times when our friend is mourning. Maybe she's experiencing loss of some sort. I've heard from friends who've lost close family members themselves that, though you can never take away the pain, you can still help a lot by letting her know you're available to listen to her, to cry with her, and occasionally, if she requests it, to distract her with something fun.

4. *Speak the truth in love.* The truth is always the best way to go—even when it's not entirely pleasant to hear. Ephesians 4:15 talks about

speaking the truth in love. With our heart set on our friend's best interest and relationship with Christ, telling her the truth of God's Word is a true friend's duty as a sister in Christ. If a friend is living in sin or walking into something harmful, withholding the truth from her simply because we fear offending her is not the loving thing to do. Definitely think, pray, and seek wise counsel before a major confrontation, but remember that a true friend loves, and love "rejoices with the truth" (1 Corinthians 13:6).

5. *Be loyal.* Loyalty means being there for our friends, even if time has gotten in the way. Proverbs 17:17 says, "A friend loves at all times, and a brother is born for adversity." Loyalty means being dependable. Our friend may not have seen us in thirteen months, but she knows who to call if she needs advice, a ride, or that certain necklace to wear to her violin recital. She knows she can depend on us to keep that surprise a secret, to finish our part of the project, and to keep our word. We may have other friends, but she knows we won't abandon her.

6. *Give her space.* Overfamiliarity can erode relationships, even between BFFs. Proverbs 25:17 warns against overstaying our welcome. Learn how to gauge when a friend wants to hang out and when she needs some time alone. Let her spend time with her other friends and her family. Just because there are other people in her life doesn't mean she's forgotten us! Time apart can be healthy for a friendship—and it makes the reunion that much sweeter!

7. *Encourage one another.* We can use our words to lift up a friend. We can thank her for how the Lord has used her in our life. We can help her stand strong in her convictions and in the Lord, reminding her of God's faithful promises. We can affirm her identity in Christ when she has doubts. We can pray for her.

8. *Be genuine.* Honesty is the only way to conduct a healthy friendship. We must love our friend for who she is, not the kind of money her family has, the status she holds, or the popularity or whatever it is she can

offer. Learning to love others for who they are instead of what they have will set us apart from the majority of the world. Be genuine about who you are, and let your friends see the real, beautiful you that God loves, not just your accomplishments and background.

9. *Give life; don't drain life.* Invest in others. Help them to live life abundantly in Jesus (John 10:10). Be that breath of fresh air that always thanks and never complains, encourages and never insults, praises more than criticizes, brightens the room instead of pulling the mood down, and stands up for what's right. When our friend is weary, she knows she can count on us to bring energy, life, and joy into her world, because we bear the sweet and brilliant light of Jesus in us (John 8:12).

10. *Point her to the Lord.* Finally, a good, true friend will point others to God. We really can't offer much of anything without Jesus, and He is ultimately the One to be glorified. He deserves it all. A successful friendship looks like two people who have grown closer to God and love Jesus more because of each other. Live out the truth with your words, actions, and thoughts. Talk about your walk with the Lord. Study God's Word, pray, and set an example with your life. And know that before anyone else, Jesus comes first, because He is our very best friend.

PERSONAL (OR GROUP) QUESTIONS

1. Who exemplifies godly friendship in your life? What have you learned from them about being a good friend?

2. What is the hardest part of maintaining a godly friendship? How can you pray for your relationships with others?

3. Which one of the ten friendship tips would you say you have done well? What is one you can work on?

Today's Challenge

Ask the Lord to bring to mind a friend whom you can spontaneously bless and encourage in her walk with Christ.

A friend loves all times...
PROV~
ERBS
17:
17

Picking Good Friends

Whoever walks with the wise becomes wise,
but the companion of fools will suffer harm.

PROVERBS 13:20 ESV

As an extrovert through and through, I thrive on a buzzing social life. You should have seen me on my first day ever of school—there were no tears or clinging to my parents' necks begging them not to leave. I had already made a new best friend in less than five minutes; I knew I was going to *relish* school. If it were up to me, I'd be friends with 96 percent of everyone. But as you have probably learned through the years like I did, we can't be friends with *everybody*. Friends come for a reason and for a season. Some cycle in and out, others stay for a while longer; dynamics change, people change. It's not a bad thing, actually. In fact, that's the beauty of God-centered friendship: God brings people into our lives and us into theirs for specific purposes. Some friendships aren't meant to last forever, and that's okay. God has a knack for providing at just the right time.

What is friendship anyway? For Christians, it should be a sort of "joining forces" for the kingdom of heaven. Powered by the loving-kindness of Christ and the mutual mission to serve Jesus, friends should seek to draw one another closer to Christ through their interactions as spiritual siblings. We have fun together, we encourage one another, we enjoy an iron-sharpening-iron kind of relationship (Proverbs 27:17).

We are sharpened because of influence—the strong power that we all possess to sway the decisions and opinions of those around us. People are moldable and inclined to emulate one another; we rub off on one another. In the right context, this is a good thing. As the body of Christ, we should "consider how to stimulate one another to love and good deeds, not forsaking our own assembling together. . .

but encouraging one another" (Hebrews 10:24–25). I guess that's what we call peer pressure—but this is the positive, redeemed angle of it.

Unfortunately, few of us are strangers to negative peer pressure. Run with the wrong crowd and don't be surprised if they overrun us. We can slowly give away our morals and make compromises as a result of allowing ourselves to be infected by wrong and ungodly ideas, lifestyles, decisions, and mindsets. Friends and other influences can draw us closer to God, but they can also draw us away from Him. In 1 Kings 11:1–3, we read how wise King Solomon made the unwise decision to marry hundreds upon hundreds of ungodly women who worshipped other gods, not thinking they would lead his heart away from the Lord.

We truly must watch the company we keep. Of course we should respect others and show the love of Christ in the way we treat them, always pointing others to Jesus and His saving Gospel, but we most certainly are not called to be bosom buddies with every person we come across. Read how Paul so passionately puts it: "Now we command you, brethren, in the name of our Lord Jesus Christ, that you keep away from every brother who leads an unruly life and not according to the tradition which you received from us" (2 Thessalonians 3:6).

We must vigilantly guard who and what we allow to influence us. Be careful about who you get close to and what you constantly feed your entertainment appetite with, because influence is no joking matter. The wrong influences can cause us to take an ugly leap off the deep end if we don't filter everything—I'm gonna say it again, but it's the whole truth—*through the Word of God.* Period.

So. . .friends: they come in all shapes, sizes, and levels. Here are some of the "ranks" of friendship:

- *Besties.* Those people we're closest to—our tightest squad, our friends-like-family. Best friends should be like-minded girls who encourage us in our walk with Christ and in following God's Word. They have our backs, and we are mutually uplifted by a close, God-honoring relationship.
- *Good friends and casual friends.* As with our best friends, our choice of our good friends says a lot about who *we* are, because we are influenced most by

those who have a direct voice into our lives.

- *Acquaintances.* We might not know them very well, but we know them and like them enough that it wouldn't be awkward if we added them on social media.

- *Ministry friends.* These are people God has brought across our path and in whose lives we have the opportunity to be a good influence. With these friends, we feel the Holy Spirit leading us to point them to Christ. While we show them the love of Christ, we also must exercise discretion, making sure we are the influencers rather than the other way around so that we don't fall into sin or stray onto the wrong path. Seek the Lord and seek counsel before deeply engaging in this category of friendship.

- *Mentors.* Pick these with extreme care! Mentors are the older friends we allow to directly speak into our lives with the explicit purpose of setting an example for us and giving us counsel and advice. Preferably, your first mentors should be your parents; other one-on-one mentors should be trusted, godly, Christian women who fear, love, and serve the Lord and prayerfully heed His Word. It could be a big sister–type mentorship, going out to ice cream with a godly Christian girl who's a little older than you (or maybe she is your literal big sister!). Or maybe she's a seasoned older woman with rich wisdom to share from her many experiences. Maybe she's a lady from your church who takes you out for coffee or a smoothie once in a while to chat.

Influence will sway who we become, whether we are shaped by friends or by other things, such as movies, books, music, or even celebrities. Is the entertainment we choose to fill ourselves with and follow wholesome and God honoring? Does it value biblical principles, or does it vouch for things that God explicitly calls evil and even hates? Does it celebrate the sin that Jesus died on the cross to overcome? Be careful about role models—are they people striving to be more loving, more truthful, more Christlike? Of course it's unpopular to look at things that way. Even many Christians do whatever the mainstream is doing, but the Lord calls us to be different by loving and following His Word! We guard what we allow into our lives because we know it does matter—we know that what we surround ourselves with will eventually begin to change us, for better or for worse.

Now, I know we've been talking a lot about picking the right kinds of friends, but maybe you're at a place where you're wondering if there are even any good friends around, much less in your life right now. I feel ya, sister. Sometimes we go through seasons when friendships are changing or there just don't seem to be any close, solid friends to call on. Use these times to grow close to God and to your family and to pray that the Lord brings you some godly, uplifting friends. I've tried it and it works: I feel lonely, I pray for a friend, and the Lord provides the right company for the right time. God cares for us like that.

Friends should be chosen not for popularity or personal gain but for mutual connection and with the purpose of drawing closer to the Lord through fellowship with His children. Friendship takes two. Pursue those wholesome relationships that reach back in shared interest. Look for good friends and always be a good friend. Show the love of Christ and set an example for the world to see. How can we help but be a good friend to others when we have a best friend like Jesus?

PERSONAL (OR GROUP) QUESTIONS

1. How are you most influenced by others? What is the hardest thing about picking influences wisely?
2. It's healthy to have a balance of all five types of friendships. What kinds of friendships has the Lord placed in your life for this season?
3. How do you benefit most from godly Christian community? Who are your main influences right now?

Today's Challenge

Pray that the Lord would bring you godly mentors and influences to spur you on toward a deeper relationship with Christ.

Whoever WALKS with the WISE becomes WISE, but the COMPANION of FOOLS will suffer harm.

PROVERBS THIRTEEN:TWENTY

Being a Good Sister

Behold, how good and how pleasant it is for
brothers [and sisters] to dwell together in unity!
PSALM 133:1

This is what happens when someone who is less than perfect tries her hand at writing a book: after writing chapter after chapter on a wide variety of topics, she comes to the chapter about being a good sister and halts. *Wait. . .I'm not always a very good sister. I still haven't mastered this by a long shot. I'm not a perfect sister, so why would I write a chapter like this?* The excuses tumble through her mind until at last she comes to a profound realization: she doesn't have *any* of these topics mastered. She is, in fact, quite imperfect. She hasn't "arrived" yet. She recognizes that each time she writes, she is really learning herself—she grows as she explores God's Word and reflects on it.

So there's my disclaimer. I am still working on my relationships with my four younger sisters, still learning to be at peace and show love and respect rather than to bicker and behave in discord. We're all still learning to direct the Latina passion and feminine drama in our strong personalities into worthwhile causes (like the theater)—not into petty arguments about who gets to sit in the front seat of the car. Nope, not perfect, but learning to apply Romans 12:18 (NIV) in my day-to-day life: "If it is possible, as far as it depends on you, live at peace with everyone." A tough challenge for such a short verse! Oftentimes, the process to restore peace in a relationship torn by war is a long one. Nevertheless, this biblical mandate is unavoidable, whether you're an only child or you have more siblings than you can count on your hands.

It's easy to be kind, loving, and peaceful with our friends. In general, they only see our "nice" side, and we pretty much only see theirs. We aren't around them 24-7, and they treat us like any decent person would treat someone—with respect, dignity, and kindness. But have you noticed how our family relationships seem the most susceptible to strain and attack? Has it crossed your mind that perhaps Satan is specifically targeting these relationships and trying to stir up trouble there?

Could it be that our family relationships are some of the most important ones ever that God has placed in our lives? So powerful and full of potential that the devil himself feels threatened by them and tries everything in his power to turn us against each other? Our God is a God of unity, and you'd better believe that Satan wants to get in the way of anything and everything God loves and values—such as our families. God Himself fashioned the very family unit that is under attack today.

We can do our part to bring peace to our home. Regardless of the people around us, we can strive to be good sisters and daughters. Psalm 133:1 says, "Behold, how good and how pleasant it is for brothers [and sisters] to dwell together in unity!" Maybe you already have a good relationship with your siblings—continue to find ways to be a dependable friend and encourager to them. Maybe your relationship is okay, but it could be better. Or maybe your sibling relationships are in desperate need of help. I have no idea, but I do know that God calls us to unity and harmony with one another, as His church and as Christians demonstrating the love of Christ.

But exercising humility and picking our arguments isn't easy: it means letting the opposing party win the battle sometimes. It means learning to give praise ten times more often than criticism, no matter the ratio we receive in return. We must learn to bring out their gold—the absolute best—rather than their "ugly side." Sometimes our siblings can bring out the worst in us, ultimately revealing our true colors. Who are we when our patience is tested? When someone messes up the room we spent hours cleaning and ruins our new rug? When someone takes for granted a kind effort we made and never even says thank you? When someone is getting on our nerves, maybe on purpose? How do we respond—will we apply the teachings of Jesus (as in Matthew 7:12), or will we lash out in annoyance, full of the flesh?

Here's the truth: it's no accident we have the siblings we do, in the birth order we're in. All of these details are intentional moves by God. Our sibling relationships have the potential to be our best friendships of all—our siblings will always be family, after all, even if we decide to waste our chance. And they need us. They need our friendship, our teamwork, and the security of our sibling bond; otherwise, they will go looking for those things outside of the family, often in places where they shouldn't be.

Are you an older sister? Me, too. My younger siblings need me to stop going with my instinctive firstborn bossiness and start being an encourager. They need me to praise them and spur them on to try new things, to be the best person God has made them to be, and to follow His exciting plan for their life. They can do without my belittling, lording over, and patronizing. They need me to be a humble leader setting a godly example. They need my listening ears, my affirming words, my thoughtfulness, and my joy. They need my prayers.

In any relationship, humility and communication contribute to peace. Whenever we have a disagreement with our siblings, we can find a kind way to sort things out (like we would with a friend or acquaintance). If, for some reason, a third party needs to get involved, let your parents or a trusted Christian adult know about the issue. There is never a need to malign our siblings to our friends.

Proverbs 18:19 says, "A brother offended is harder to be won than a strong city." Often our familiarity causes us to treat our family members with less respect than other people. It shouldn't be this way; we read in God's Word that "a friend is always loyal, and a brother is born to help in time of need" (Proverbs 17:17 NLT). Unfortunately, offenses are hard to recover from. A good relationship won't just happen—it takes fierce intention. We need to want a good relationship with our siblings and work at becoming a better sister every day, through every interaction, if we want to see a mediocre or bad relationship transform.

But listen, there is hope—no matter how many years we've spent squabbling with, competing with, putting down, or brushing aside our siblings, God delights in transforming things from bad to good. Ask the Lord to give you a tender heart toward your family. Let Him convict and change you. We can begin working on our own flaws instead of nitpicking our siblings' flaws (Matthew 7:5). We can pray for our siblings by name; we'll find it's just too hard to have enmity toward them in our hearts if we are constantly praying that God blesses them abundantly and works in their lives.

So pray—and be proactive about getting your good sister game on, winning your siblings over by showing deep, fervent loving-kindness like Christ has shown to us. Love them right where they are. Show them love in the meaningful ways that you know they will receive.

I want to be that sister who doesn't waste the opportunity to invest in her siblings' lives. I want to seek after a good relationship and win their friendship. Think twenty years from now—who knows how many of our current friends will still be around? Friendships change, but family is always family. Many of us take that for granted; we didn't choose these people we call siblings, after all. But God did. He handpicked my sisters—Genevieve, Melody, Harmony, and Felicity—and He has a fantastic plan behind it all. Realize the gift God has given you. Life is never guaranteed, so take each moment to say, "I love you," and cherish the truly important blessings God has given you. That's my challenge for you and for me.

PERSONAL (OR GROUP) QUESTIONS

1. What is your main sibling struggle? Pinpoint the problem that bothers you most; what do you think is the root of the issue?

2. How can you respond in love and work toward bringing out the best in those around you, even if they don't make an effort?

3. Have you played a part in stirring up strife in your family? What steps can you take to restore peace?

Today's Challenge

Write out three things you love and three prayer points for each of your siblings. Take them before the Lord and ask that He bring peace, unity, love, and friendship to your family, strengthening or even restoring your relationships.

Behold, HOW GOOD & how PLEASANT it is for brothers AND sisters to DWELL together in unity! PSALM 133:1

Submitting to Authority

Children, obey your parents in the Lord, for this is right. Honor your father and mother (which is the first commandment with a promise), so that it may be well with you, and that you may live long on the earth.
Ephesians 6:1–3

Welcome to a world trying to establish only one rule: *There are no rules. And no one should tell you what to do,* they say. Feeling a little rebellious today? Try respecting authority—it goes against everything our culture's preaching at us. Most of us have forgotten that authority, designed by the Lord, is inescapable. No matter who we are, what we do, where we rank, or whether we ourselves hold an authoritative position, we are always responding to a higher power. Romans 13:1 makes a case for the wisdom of obeying authority: "Every person is to be in subjection to the governing authorities. For there is no authority except from God, and those which exist are established by God." No human can evade authority—the highest authority, after all, is God Himself.

When we surrender our life to Jesus, we give up our "right" to run life our way. We give Him authority over our whole life. We submit to His will. We obey His commandments. We make Him Lord. Galatians 1:10 talks about our being "bond-servant[s] of Christ" who desire to please the Lord. The ironic thing about surrendering our rights is that as we become "slaves of righteousness" (Romans 6:18), there we find the truest freedom (John 8:36).

So what is meant by this broad term, "authority"? It can include anyone from world leaders and presidents to police officers, teachers, employers, you name it, but more than likely, you and I have two main authorities in our lives who hit pretty close to home: our parents. That's right, Mom and Dad themselves. The two people out of all the billions on the planet whom God handpicked to bring us to life.

Disclaimer: I realize there are a lot of crazy and not-so-ideal family situations out there. I don't know your situation, but I do know that the Lord commands us to honor our father and mother (Exodus 20:12)—that doesn't mean, however, that we have to obey ungodly commands. If authority looks like guardians, relatives, or other adults in your life, remember that the Lord will give us the grace and strength to handle any situation if we ask for His help. God never makes mistakes—life, circumstances, and family members are never by accident. Our parents deserve our honor, even if only for the fact that they brought us into this world.

"Children, obey your parents in the Lord, for this is right. Honor your father and mother (which is the first commandment with a promise), so that it may be well with you, and that you may live long on the earth" (Ephesians 6:1–3). This scripture clues us in on a golden life principle: God honors us when we choose to honor our parents. Honor is a step above respect—we ought to respect everyone by treating them properly, with dignity. Honor regards someone as important, special, and highly ranked. It goes out of its way to give, do, and say only the best. It holds a person in a respectable place and never, ever maligns that person.

It's easy to forget that honoring our parents is a commandment, not just a good idea. When God gives commandments, He does so for a reason. He doesn't abuse His authority, but rather He truly wants us to live dynamic lives by His side. He expects us to obey Him because we trust Him, even if we don't understand. When He says "do" or "don't do" something, He's being a good parent, directing His children to the best and helping us avoid the worst.

God gave us our specific parents for a reason. More than likely, He desires to use them as some of the most significant voices in our lives. Parents can be counselors, teachers, spiritual mentors, encouragers, disciplinarians, caretakers, comforters, and friends. They are the first earthly authority the Lord places in our lives. I have been blessed with godly parents who love me and love each other. They have molded my life greatly. I truly would not be where I am today (I wouldn't *be* at all!) if it weren't for them. Get to know your parents. Scrutinize your life and don't overlook the sacrifices they've made for you. What kinds of investments have they poured into your life?

Every set of parents is different, and every family's standards vary. Did you ever have that one friend whose parents were "super strict" and never let her do or watch anything? Yep, that was me. Flash back to when I was thirteen and the youth group girls were having a conversation about strict parents with the youth pastor's wife. In this discussion, my sweet friend piped up, "Well, when I complain to my mom about her rules, she says, 'Just be thankful you don't have Marjorie's mom!'"

Gulp. One of my favorite awkward moments of my adolescence—and yes, said friend and I are still friends. And she was right, my parents did set a lot of boundaries for me and my sisters—a few that I resented at the time. But as I've climbed through my teen years, I've come to realize that most of their "rules" were really very smart. Looking back, I'm extremely grateful for their guidance and wouldn't have it any other way. Where many of my peers had unrestrained freedom, my parents placed strict accountability. In a rampantly materialistic world, my parents chose to withhold some of the trivial luxuries every nine-year-old in my class had (like cell phones, laptops and all sorts of other expensive electronics I craved). Obeying and honoring authority was tough when all I saw was the fun I was missing. But now, realizing those rules were in place because of my parents' love and care, realizing how much I *did not* miss, realizing how much good those rules did me, I am relieved and thankful.

We're growing up in a "you're-not-the-boss-of-me" generation. People of our generation see unreasonable rules established by unreasonable people and decide to ditch them altogether so they can "do their own thing," express their "individuality." Rebellion is an epidemic that is wiping people out—it's dangerous, foolish, and contagious. Not to mention, the rejection of authority—set in place by God—is downright sinful: "For rebellion is as the sin of witchcraft" (1 Samuel 15:23 NKJV). *Suppose* our parents are "unreasonable." Nowhere in scripture are we exempt from obedience, other than in the face of wicked commands. I have seen good Christian girls and role models rebel against their parents with the excuse that their parents' rules were "unreasonable" or "unfair"—and go on to do something rash like marry a guy who "loved them more" without their parents' blessing (which is extremely important). That saddens me—that girls like you and me could ignore the Lord's commands, listen to lies, and make poor decisions they will eventually majorly regret.

Earthly authority isn't perfect—it's true that parents do fail sometimes. They make mistakes, they have their flaws, but so do we. Extend grace to your family, to Mom and Dad, and focus on fostering a relationship of love, honor, forgiveness, trust, and openness. One of the greatest things my parents have done for me is established that I can talk to them about *anything* and everything. We have awkward conversations about awkward, sweat-inducing topics. We have tear-filled confessions and heart-to-hearts. We have not only a good therapist-client relationship but also a solid friendship.

Submission is one of those words that offends people quickly, because we hate the idea of giving up our rights, not being in charge, and letting someone else have the final say. There are plenty of people whose actions give submission a bad name, but in reality, it was meant to be beautiful. Submission is the story of salvation—Jesus submitted Himself to His Father's will and died for us. We submit ourselves to Jesus through repentance and trust in salvation. Right now, our joy is to submit to the parents (and possibly other authorities) the Lord has placed in our lives. Someday, that authority will transfer over to our husband in the beautiful marriage picture of the bride of Christ submitting to her Groom, Jesus, who gave Himself entirely to her. And always, we first and foremost submit to God, because He is the perfect authority, and He has only good thoughts toward us (Jeremiah 29:11).

PERSONAL (OR GROUP) QUESTIONS

1. Who are some of the authorities in your life? Are you in a position of authority yourself?

2. What are some standards that authorities in your life have set? What is it like to obey them?

3. What rules or standards in your life are you most grateful for? Why?

Today's Challenge

Find a way to intentionally honor your parents today. Maybe through a gift, a kind note, an encouraging word, a helping hand, or a gesture of friendship. Pray that the Lord will work in your relationship with your parents and give you the humility to joyfully submit to authority.

Being Teachable

Listen to counsel and accept discipline,
that you may be wise the rest of your days.
PROVERBS 19:20

Did you ever try to learn something that just did not, could not, would not stick? That was the story of me and high school chemistry. Chemistry and I, we were not friends. I cried my way through, got weekly tutoring from a kind (and brilliant) classmate, and made it out barely alive with a good grade. One year later, here I am writing this with *zero* recollection of anything I learned in that class—except to *never* take a chemistry class again. I have an increased respect for people whose brains compute—and even enjoy—when math and science collide.

Thankfully, there have been many other classes, subjects, and lessons in my life that have stuck in my mind better than chemistry did. Good thing, too, because I love to learn and grow. It's a natural, thrilling part of life—as we learn, we grow and have the potential to become better people. The more wisdom and understanding we have, the less likely we are to make a bad decision. When we do make mistakes, we can learn valuable lessons.

Every single day the Lord is speaking to us and teaching us. Like the good Father He is to His children, He wants us to grow and become more equipped for the life He has planned for us. God is a creative teacher—He chooses to teach us many different ways. Some ways are pleasant; others are trying. Some teachings we like; some we might not. Some lessons are quick and easy; some are long and grueling. Some lessons may be challenges to surge us up onto the next level, while others may be remedial or correctional lessons that prune us of ungodly character. Some lessons help us to confront our flaws here and there, and others are designed to refine us under extreme pressure to change us into who God wants us to be.

We ask God to make us more and more like Christ, to help us conquer sin and temptation, to give us a heart for missions, to change us. . .but are we prepared for that change? Are we prepared to be taught, convicted, maybe even *corrected*? Are we prepared to listen with an open heart that is ready to obey the words of God? He has powerful, beautiful, true, loving words to speak to us—we need to listen up and learn to detect His voice! God has many methods He uses to teach us. Here are a few of them:

- *The Bible.* God's Word is a direct message from the Lord to us! Not only does it hold the grand history of God's hand in all the earth since creation, but each verse is there for a reason. God's Word holds every answer and truth. The more we know the Word and take it to heart, meditating on it and applying it, the more we grow. If we allow the truth of the Bible to penetrate our hearts and shine light into every corner of our lives, God's words begin to change us—we begin to live out what we have saturated our minds in.

  Often when we're reading the Bible, God will single out a specific verse or passage to share with us. The still, small voice of the Holy Spirit will prick our hearts with a specific thought from God bearing a direct application to us. Maybe it's an encouragement—like a pat on the back. Maybe it's a correction—we read a verse and suddenly become convicted of sin in that area of our life. Conviction is good, because through it we have the opportunity to grow, even though there is remorse over sin. More on that in a second, though. Maybe God's word to us is an answer to something we've been praying about. Or maybe He is teaching us a lesson that strikes a chord within us and tunes our hearts in the right direction.

- *Circumstances and situations.* God never puts us anywhere by accident. Whatever country, city, school, workplace, or family He has put us in is an intentional move on His part. While God never harms us, He does allow bad things to happen sometimes. We don't always understand His ways, and sometimes we go through pain. Yet how comforting and hopeful to realize that even though we have to walk through trials, hardships, and even fire sometimes in life, He is there with us, and our pain is never for nothing. In fact, grief and suffering, depending on our response, have the potential to draw us close to God in a way we never could have experienced in an easy-breezy life. He lovingly teaches us lessons such as depending on Him, recognizing the brevity of life and making each moment count, loving well those He has placed in our lives, and learning what matters most.

On the flip side, there is no limit to the kinds of situations and circumstances God can teach us through. Hard times like the death of a loved one, a long-distance move, and other difficulties are indeed full of lessons, but God uses joyful times as well to teach us. Attend a God-centered wedding, and be blown away by the beautiful characteristics of marriage that parallel God's tremendous love for His church! God can teach us through nature—see His lesson on trusting Him to provide in Matthew 6:27–29. Experiencing the joy of family, witnessing true neighborliness—there are so many ways God can teach and speak His sweet words to us.

- *People.* God can use someone's encouragement, conversation, gift, writing, bit of advice, wise counsel, or even rebuke or confrontation to teach us or speak to us. This is not to say that every kind word or criticism is from the Lord; we ought to filter everything spoken to us through prayer and scripture. God's Word is grounded in truth, not just people's opinions. His words, though immovable and straightforward, are full of hope and the desire to bring us to a place where we can experience His love, grace, and freedom with joy. With that in mind, never put it above the Lord to use the authorities and influences around us, like parents, pastors, mentors, counselors, even godly friends and siblings, to speak into our lives.

But let's face it, we young people as a whole aren't a very teachable bunch. Few people embrace correction and instruction. Instead, the commonly mocked "teenage attitude" says, "Don't tell me what to do." Often, taking advice or even correction poses a threat to our pride, because we have to admit that we *do* need help, we *aren't* perfect, and perhaps someone else does know something we don't, because *we don't know everything*. And admitting that is way too humbling for our tastes.

If we were trying to follow the crowd and be any old typical teen, I'd advise us to be stubborn and hard hearted—don't let anyone tell you what to do. But clearly, that way of thinking is simply foolish and blind. Just listen to what Proverbs says: "Fools despise wisdom and instruction" (Proverbs 1:7); "[A fool] will despise the wisdom of your words" (Proverbs 23:9); "The way of a fool is right in his own eyes, but a wise man is he who listens to counsel" (Proverbs 12:15).

As devoted Christ followers, we ought to embrace counsel. Though it's not pleasant to be wrong or to receive correction, we need to realize that God corrects His children because He loves us—it is an honor to be taught by God. King David implored the Lord, "Make me know Your ways, O Lord; teach me Your paths. Lead me in Your truth and teach me, for You are the God of my salvation; for You I wait all the day" (Psalm 25:4–5).

When we learn to be teachable and correctable and even to embrace conviction, we will begin to have spiritual growth spurts. God is all about shedding light on the dark spots in our lives. Once we realize the sin we still have in our lives, we repent and become more dependent on Christ so that He can work in and through us. Here's the difference between conviction and condemnation: *condemnation* points a blaming finger, inflicts guilt and shame, and says, *There is no hope for you. This sin is who you are. You can never change.* In contrast, *conviction* is straight from the Holy Spirit. It's like a heart prick within. Yes, it may sting and feel a little like guilt sometimes, but conviction bears hope—it's for our good. It doesn't tamper with the fact that God loves us completely, always and forever. Conviction is given so that we can get better—because this sin is *not* who we are; it's only who we've become. And that can change, because God will restore us if we repent and allow Him to.

Desire God's wisdom and spiritual growth. Seek out wise counsel from a godly older woman in your life—someone who can pour sound biblical truth and advice into your life, encouraging you to live in obedience to Jesus. Listen to her words. Read biblically sound books and study up on scripture. Look around your life for God's lessons to you. Wisdom is priceless—"How much better it is to get wisdom than gold!" (Proverbs 16:16).

PERSONAL (OR GROUP) QUESTIONS

1. What is your response to correction? What about conviction?

2. What is the best counsel you've ever received?

3. Who are some of the godly voices the Lord has provided to speak into your life? Are you a voice of sound, godly counsel in someone else's life?

Today's Challenge

Ask the Lord to speak to you and teach you. Pray that He would point out areas of needed growth in your life and direct you in His ways (Psalm 23:3).

PROVERBS 19:TWENTY

Listen to counsel & accept discipline

that you may be WISE the rest of your days

DAY 29

Living Wisely

"For wisdom is better than jewels; and all desirable things cannot compare with her."

PROVERBS 8:11

The book of Proverbs makes a compelling case for a competitive offer—wisdom—like a lengthy infomercial with all sorts of benefits if you act now: Valued at "more precious than jewels" (Proverbs 3:15), wisdom is a rare but necessary quality in any Christian's life. But wait—there's more. If you ask now, you can get wisdom absolutely free (those who are faithless and doubting are excluded from the discount—James 1:5–6). Wisdom is guaranteed to be a "tree of life to those who take hold of her, and happy are all who hold her fast" (Proverbs 3:18). Wisdom is hands down better than its competitor, foolishness. Call to the Lord to get your free wisdom today.

Cheesy, I know—but read through the book of Proverbs, and you'll see it's not at all a far cry from the truth. Verse after verse and chapter after chapter, the writer continually pushes the importance of getting wisdom. "Do not forsake [wisdom], and she will guard you; love her, and she will watch over you" (Proverbs 4:6). See what I mean? There is so much emphasis on living life wisely.

You see, we've been entrusted with this amazing gift—life—and are responsible for taking care of it. You know what they say—we only live once. That means we only have one shot. Don't you think we should aim to get it right the first time? The concept of stewardship is expressed in Luke 12:35–48, a passage that reminds us to take faithful care of the responsibilities God has entrusted to us. To be devoted to the end.

As God's daughters, we are also His representatives (2 Corinthians 5:20); children do reflect their families and their parents, after all. What message does our life send to those around us? Is our reputation one of Christlike love, uncompromised truth, godliness, character. . .or are there people who have valid complaints to give a negative review about who we are? Proverbs 22:1 puts weight to the value of our reputation: "A good name is to be more desired than great wealth, favor is better than silver and gold." Our reputation affects our testimony—the story of what God has done and is doing in our life. To be an effective witness to the life-changing Gospel, we have to live out that life change!

A good reputation is often a reflection of the consistency of our character. So far as we have any say in it, we should be known for living in a God-honoring way. Sometimes, however, things outside of our control happen—perhaps someone with evil and selfish intentions tries to attack our reputation. Remember that ultimately, God has our reputation in His hands. The truth always wins in the end—in this life or in the next. What's important is that our reputation before God is one of purity and holiness.

Living wisely and responsibly, however, is not limited to what others see in our lives. In fact, obeying God starts with what people don't see. Seeking the Lord full speed ahead as our number one priority is the wisest move we can make in this life. We need Him desperately, and we'd do well to acknowledge that.

We know that God has an amazing, comprehensive plan for our lives, and we want to receive His blessings to the fullest. Sadly, young people often choose to have a narrow view of their lives rather than keeping their future in mind. They choose to live it up in their youth, partying hardy and enjoying temporary pleasures, thinking a spree of wild living won't be a big deal. Fast-forward ten or fifteen years to a million and one regrets as many of these people spend their adulthood trying to clean up their mess of a life. Thinking about our actions instead of following the whims of our hormones and impulses will save us loads of trouble and please the Lord. It is one of the ways we say, "I trust You, Lord. I know Your plans are far bigger and better than a fleeting experience."

As we grow in the Lord, we learn the wisdom of seeking Him first before making decisions. Learn to hear His kind voice. As we heed the Holy Spirit's leading in our hearts and the sound counsel of wise Christians, we begin to realize that God wants to be involved in every area of our lives—in every decision we make. Why? Because He wants His best for us. Sometimes on our own judgment, we settle for second best, or we miss a detail. But God directs us by paving a specific path for us to take. Who needs Siri when you're in tune with the Holy Spirit's direction?

We need to get to know God's Holy Spirit in us. Did you know that it is through His power that we can resist sin and temptation? Don't be fooled—sin and temptation are real and are hard at work, even with good Christian girls. The enemy is trying to slay us all. He wants to mar our reputation, thwart our testimony, stain our purity, ruin our witness, darken our future, and destroy our soul.

A truly wise person retains this golden nugget of advice: *Never put yourself above sin.* The moment we say, "Well, I could *never* do that," is the moment we let down our guard and allow compromise, and before we know it, that silent killer called sin has taken us. Believe it—sin has slain the best of professing believers. How did it happen? Trace it back—it started in the secrecy of their hearts. You see, there is a direct link from the thoughts we allow ourselves to entertain in our hearts and minds to the verbal and physical actions we take. In other words, what's going on in secret won't stay secret forever.

It is devastating to see someone whose life was going so well suddenly crash and burn in moral failure. Thankfully, it doesn't need to be this way. We must acknowledge that every single one of us has the capacity for the worst of sins. We really could fall if we're not careful—which is why we need to take precautions! Know your weaknesses and temptations. Have accountability in your life—one or two individuals (preferably your parents or another trusted Christian adult) with whom you share everything. You put all your dirty laundry on the table so it's out in the open. You get it off your chest, and it can no longer thrive in the quiet of the dark. The light—God's light—kills the dark. There is great freedom in speaking the truth and in shedding light on sin and exposing it.

First Thessalonians 5:5 describes believers as "sons of light and sons of day." In other words, our lives in public ought to be consistent with our lives in private. We are the same people through and through. We live with integrity, doing the right thing even when nobody's watching—because we know that Somebody is always watching us.

"Be wise in what is good and innocent in what is evil": Romans 16:19 leaves us with a life challenge. An ongoing battle is raging for our purity, our love, our allegiance, our minds, and our hearts. Without wisdom, we have no hope of advancing in the fight. Get wisdom, and get humility—the two go hand in hand. What a beautiful responsibility it is to use God's breath of life in our lungs with purpose. Don't waste the priceless gift you've been given—choose wisdom.

PERSONAL (OR GROUP) QUESTIONS

1. Who in your life or in the Bible is an example of wisdom? How has wisdom blessed this person's life?

2. If others were to describe you in three words, what would they say? What are some ways your reputation can point others to Christ?

3. Think of a time when you sought the Lord for an answer and you heard Him. Describe that experience.

Today's Challenge

Read the Proverbs chapter of the day. (Is today the fourteenth? Read chapter 14.) Memorize a verse of your choice from the chapter.

For wisdom is better than jewels and all desirable things cannot compare with her

Proverbs 8:11

Determining God's Will

*"Call to Me and I will answer you, and I will tell you
great and mighty things, which you do not know."*
JEREMIAH 33:3

Chocolate chip cookie dough or cappuccino-flavored ice cream? Should I buy this car or that one? College A or College B? Should I wear the blue shirt or the green shirt? Decisions, decisions. Life is full of them. I confess, making decisions is my weak point. I have a history of indecisive waffling—and I especially don't like making a big decision under timed pressure. You see, I often fear making the wrong choice and messing up God's plan for my life. Does the unknown scare or excite you? For me, it's both. Life is riddled with unknowns, and sometimes it feels like we're moving forward without actually being able to see where we're headed. And that can be a strange emotional mixture of thrilling and discouraging.

As Christians, we want to seek God's will and trust His plan, but *what exactly is He doing?* Where are we going? Are we going to like it? Are we going to miss (or mess up) God's will? Are we going to be happy or lonely? The questions swirling through our minds are enough to send us into a panic. How do we make the right decisions, discern God's will, and hear His voice?

Our teenage years are a pivotal time in our lives. We have big decisions to make, hopes and dreams we'd like to fulfill. We may be considering school, college, majors, jobs, friendships, travel, marriage, and mission opportunities. God is leading us into something new, but often, letting go of the past and boldly venturing into God's plan for us takes all kinds of courage. We usually can't see very far around the bend, and rarely do we drive by a billboard that spells out God's will for us. How, then, do we know what decisions God wants us to make when we can't see His full, eternal view?

We pray to God—but how often do we *listen* to Him? He always has something to say to us, and His words are loving, kind, beautiful, and for our edification. The Lord desires to be involved in our decisions because, being the good Father He is, He cares about us and wants to lead us into His fulfilling purpose and calling for our lives.

If we're wanting to move forward with a big decision, we'd best be sure we know God is behind it. But how do we know we've heard from God? We might not hear an audible voice reverberating off our eardrum. Rather, perk up your spiritual eyes and ears (Acts 28:27), because God often speaks to us through the following methods:

- *His Word.* God speaks to us through His Word, the Bible, and He handpicks passages to spring off the page and apply directly to us. Disclaimer: anything and everything God says will always line up with the Bible and will never contradict it. Contradictions are a surefire way to recognize a voice that *isn't* God's!
- *People.* The Lord can use wise, godly counsel from our parents or other trusted Christian mentors and leaders in our life to speak to us. Perhaps a sermon wakes us up to the truth, or a bit of advice registers with the questions we've been asking. A timely word can help shift us in the right direction. Of course, even the best of folks are human, so test every word spoken to you through prayer and scripture.
- *Peace.* God often uses a profound peace (or lack thereof) given by His Holy Spirit in us. Remember, there's a difference between "peace" and "happiness." There have been times when I wasn't necessarily happy with where I believed God was directing me, but I had a confirming, restful peace within me. The Holy Spirit brings peace; anything short of that is a blaring alarm that a problem needs to be addressed. Constant wavering without a steady peace can also indicate that something's wrong.
- *The Holy Spirit.* Sometimes as we're reading God's Word, quietly meditating on scripture, going about our day, or trying to fall asleep, we hear a

calming voice, so "still" and "small," speak to our hearts. Sometimes it can feel a bit like our conscience assuring or warning us. It's nothing spooky or weird—you know when you hear the voice of the Holy Spirit speak a specific word to your heart. His voice is authoritative yet sweet, true, comforting, and restful.

- *Opportunities.* The Lord can direct us through our situation or circumstances. He can open and shut doors of opportunity, hand carving a course for us to take. As we prayerfully step forward onto those glowing stepping-stones we believe God is illuminating before us, we may discover a blocked path. A closed door. That avenue has been closed off. God is navigating us onto a different course.

What if God is directing us somewhere we don't want to go? Like Nineveh? Jonah decided to run and attempt to hide from God when he got sent there—and he experienced some atypical consequences for his gall to disobey. He should've known it's impossible to hide from God. He'll always find us. Besides, who are we to tell God no? He knows best. He sees the bigger picture—all the lives involved, the stories interwoven, the reactions connected.

So here's a question I've wrestled with before: If I make a wrong decision, will I mess up God's plan for my life? Will my one wrong move throw me off track with God's will? It's a scary thought, because we know we're not perfect and we're bound to make mistakes! Here's where faith comes into play: I believe that God is sovereign above all and that His grace covers me and fills in the cracks where I make mistakes. God has an ultimate plan and purpose that cannot be revoked—just ask Jonah, who still ended up preaching in Nineveh even after his sprint in the opposite direction. However, as we seek God's will, abide in Him daily, and obey Him, we invite Him to be an intimate part of our everyday lives and decisions. I want to welcome God's blessings. I want to be in harmony with His grand plan and His many subplans, not do things the hard way and get swallowed up by a fish until I decide to comply.

A couple of things can hinder us from hearing God's voice. If we approach the Lord for an answer while we have blatant, unrepentant sin in our lives, we shouldn't be surprised by the wall that is blocking our communication. Distraction also can make it difficult to hear God because our mind is flying a hundred miles an hour. And sometimes we're stubborn—so fixed in our ways, opinions, and hopes that we close ourselves off to the possibility of God directing us in any way other than *our* way. But our way is never as comprehensive as God's way.

Decisions can be big, but God is always bigger. Don't worry. Worrying only leads to confusion and inhibits our ability to think straight. Instead of taking our cares to God in specific prayer (Philippians 4:6) and keeping our heart open to hear His voice, we freak out and run around in mental circles. God never fails to come through when we need Him—He's never late. He is always speaking His kind, true words and giving us Fatherly direction—but we have to admit, we aren't always listening.

Feeling apprehensive may be natural, but we can firmly choose to have faith in God's goodness, provision, will, timing, and plan. We can choose to live out that same faith by trusting that God is in control and by taking those leaps forward as we believe He is directing. Jeremiah 33:3 says, "Call to Me and I will answer you, and I will tell you great and mighty things, which you do not know." Pray about decisions! Pray about the unknown. Write out letters to God and talk to Him about your concerns. Then take a deep breath and experience the peace and freedom that come from living a life under the watchful care of One who is completely in control—the Lord Jesus.

PERSONAL (OR GROUP) QUESTIONS

1. What kinds of decisions have you had to make recently? What decisions do you have before you?

2. Describe a time when you heard God's voice. In what ways does God often speak to you?

3. What is the hardest thing about seeking God's direction? How is it beneficial?

Today's Challenge

Are you seeking direction? Wondering what decision to make? Bring your cares to the Lord and listen for His voice. Let Him be a part of your every move.

Call to Me & I will answer you & I will tell you GREAT AND mighty things WHICH YOU DO NOT KNOW

Jeremiah 33:III

Trusting God with Your Future

I would have despaired unless I had believed that I would see the goodness of the Lord in the land of the living. Wait for the Lord; be strong and let your heart take courage; yes, wait for the Lord.

PSALM 27:13–14

Shrouded in mystery and hope is the future, looming ahead in a fog of unknowns. We can't live in the past forever; we are ushered forward along the calendar every day. We can take practical steps, draw out plans, and speculate over facts, but ultimately, none of us know God's entire detailed plan for our lives from beginning to end. Proverbs 16:9 says, "The mind of man plans his way, but the LORD directs his steps." Sometimes God will reveal to us only the very next step, without showing us where we're going to land—and we're supposed to trust Him and jump.

Wouldn't it be nice to know what the future holds? To know God's complete purpose, plan, and will for the grand scheme of our life? When we invite Jesus into our hearts, our life becomes the Lord's handwritten story of His faithfulness, goodness, and glory. Chapter after chapter brings new twists, turns, blessings, surprises, and trials. Tomorrow is a day uncharted—it's anyone's guess whether there will be laughter, loneliness, pain, celebration, heartbreak, or happiness.

I wish we could "bet our bottom dollar" that "the sun'll come out tomorrow" as brightly as Annie did, but there could be a different forecast overshadowing some of the days ahead. The Bible never promises believers an easy-breezy, walking-on-sunshine life—actually, life gets hard sometimes. We have very little control over the future, whether it is blissfully euphoric or painfully difficult. We don't know for sure what will happen next week, next month, or next year—but we do know who is in control. We know who God is.

- *God is sovereign.* That means He's over all. Working outside the boundaries of space, time, reason, and possibility, He's 100 percent in control. He keeps the sun at just the right distance to support life on planet earth, He guides wars and battles, He raises up and brings down world powers—and He also tends to the beautiful lilies. Nothing slips His notice. He is the Head over all.

- *God is a good Father.* "See how great a love the Father has bestowed on us," we read in 1 John 3:1, "that we would be called children of God; and such we are." What an honor to be God's own daughters. He possesses all the qualities of a perfect dad—loving, caring, desiring our betterment, protecting, empowering, and kind.

  He may allow hardships to draw us closer to Himself, make us more like Christ, and produce character within us. But don't think for a minute that God is coldhearted, distant, and stoic. This is the Lord who offers us rest—who offers Himself as our lifelong "life support" in Matthew 11:28–30. He delights to bless us and express His love for us. In Luke 11:13 Jesus says, "If you then, being evil, know how to give good gifts to your children, how much more will your heavenly Father give the Holy Spirit to those who ask Him?" God has given us the best gift of all—His own Spirit residing within us to guide, encourage, convict, empower, and strengthen us.

- *God has a master plan.* You and I have hopes and dreams. We want to do big, important, meaningful things to change the world, make a difference, share Jesus with everyone. We want to draw closer to the Lord and know Him deeply. We want to serve the Lord and live in harmony with His perfect will. What if the route to true, godly fulfillment leads us not through the flowery fields, but through the fire? What if pressure is crushing in and squeezing us on every side? Will we break and settle for a lesser substitute of living, or will we emerge as refined diamonds and pearls?

  God's vantage point surveys a much larger chunk of the full picture than we can see from the seats we get—He sees all of eternity. We may never see the rippling effects of our obedience, faithfulness, and trust in the Lord on this side of heaven, but the Lord is meticulously strategizing and directing the events of our lives to fit perfectly like little cogs into His grand design of a plan.

- *God has a purpose for us.* If Jeremiah 1:5 doesn't blow you away, then I don't know what will: "Before I formed you in the womb I knew you, and before you were born I consecrated you." God knows us inside and out; He made us and endowed us with a divine purpose even while we were only thoughts on His mind. Psalm 139:16 says, "Your eyes have seen my unformed substance; and in Your book were all written the days that were ordained for me, when as yet there was not one of them." God knew about today before it ever happened. He knew about yesterday. He has a purpose for every event in our lives, good or bad. Sometimes, though, it takes great patience to see how He "causes all things to work together for good to those who love God, to those who are called according to His purpose" (Romans 8:28).

- *God keeps His promises.* He will never abandon us (Hebrews 13:5). He is always with us (Matthew 28:20). He will always love us (Romans 8:38–39). The Bible is brimming with promises, and God keeps every one of them. Second Peter 3:9 says, "The Lord is not slow about His promise, as some count slowness, but is patient toward you." God has His reasons for His timing. We may not understand it, but we have to trust Him with all our heart and realize that He cares. He is good. He always keeps His word.

- *God wins in the end.* The Bible depicts the epic battle of good versus evil, heaven versus hell, God versus Satan. I hope you've read the end of the book, because I'm going to spoil it for you: *God wins!* Revelation 21:5 says, "And He [Jesus] who sits on the throne said, 'Behold, I am making all things new.' " Gain an eternal perspective. Our future on earth is short; what about eternity—forever and ever? Praise the Lord, we know who's King during and after this messy life.

"Trust and obey, for there's no other way to be happy in Jesus, but to trust and obey." One of my favorite old hymns holds the key to dealing with the future ahead. It's committed trust and faithful obedience. It's confidence that we can trust God, because He is our loving Father who is always there for us.

Sure, our plans might seem good. But I want God's. Instead of clinging to our future and trying to stay in control, let's release our plans, hopes, and dreams to the Lord. They may become a reality; they may not. We may have good times, and we may have bad ones. No, we can't erase the uncertainty of the future, but we can rest securely in the peace Jesus brings. Come rain or sunshine, choose to trust God. He will direct you. He will protect you. Don't fear the future. Rather, live life abundantly and joyfully (John 10:10). *Stay devoted.*

PERSONAL (OR GROUP) QUESTIONS

1. What hopes and dreams do you have for the future? What about worries?
2. What discourages you from trusting God with your future? Why do you choose to trust God?
3. What areas of your future do you need to surrender to the Lord in prayer?

Today's Challenge

First Peter 5:7 (NKJV) says, "[Cast] all your care upon Him, for He cares for you." When you are tempted to worry, immediately shift those cares off your back and hand them over to the Lord in prayer—He's ultimately in control. The devil won't want to keep pestering you with worry if you're going to turn right around and pray every time!

I would have despaired UNLESS I had believed

that I would see the goodness of the Lord in the land of the living.

WAIT for the LORD, BE STRONG & LET YOUR ♥ TAKE COURAGE & yes, WAIT for the LORD

PSALM 27:13-14

The Smart Girl's Guide to Mean Girls, Manicures, and God's Amazing Plan for ME

by Susie Shellenberger and Kristen Weber

The Smart Girl's Guide to Mean Girls, Manicures, and God's Amazing Plan for ME melds spiritual and practical advice with humor—a winning combination for teen girls trying to navigate the ups and downs of life with grace and confidence. You'll will be encouraged and challenged with sound, biblically based advice equipping you to go deeper in your faith and grow an increasingly intimate relationship with God—plus, you'll encounter some fun, common-sense tips along the way.

Paperback / 978-1-63409-713-0 / 240 pages / $12.99

Find These and More from Shiloh Run Press at Your Favorite Bookstore Or at www.shilohrunpress.com

SHILOH RUN PRESS
An Imprint of Barbour Publishing, Inc.